# Brilliant Computer Basics

# Matt Powell

**PEARSON**

Prentice Hall

Harlow, England • London • New York • Boston • San Francisco • Toronto • Sydney • Singapore • Hong Kong
Tokyo • Seoul • Taipei • New Delhi • Cape Town • Madrid • Mexico City • Amsterdam • Munich • Paris • Milan

**Pearson Education Limited**
Edinburgh Gate
Harlow
Essex CM20 2JE
England

and Associated Companies throughout the world

*Visit us on the World Wide Web at:*
www.pearsoned.co.uk

**First published 2006**

ISBN-13: 978-0-13-188813-5
ISBN-10: 0-13-188813-7


**British Library Cataloguing-in-Publication Data**
A catalogue record for this book is available from the British Library

**Library of Congress Cataloging-in-Publication Data**
A CIP catalog record for this book can be obtained from the Library of Congress

10 9 8 7 6 5 4 3 2 1
10 09 08 07 06

Prepared for Pearson Education Ltd by Syllaba Ltd (http://www.syllaba.co.uk)
Editorial management by McNidder & Grace, Alnwick
Typeset in Helvetica LT Narrow 11pt by P.K. McBride, Southampton
Printed and bound in Great Britain by Ashford Colour Press Ltd., Gosport.

The publisher's policy is to use paper manufactured from sustainable forests.

# Brilliant guides

## What you need to know and how to do it

When you're working on your PC and come up against a problem that you're unsure how to solve, or want to accomplish something in an application that you aren't sure how to do, where do you look? Manuals and traditional training guides are usually too big and unwieldy and are intended to be used as end-to-end training resources, making it hard to get to the info you need right away without having to wade through pages of background information that you just don't need at that moment – and helplines are rarely that helpful!

*Brilliant* guides have been developed to allow you to find the info you need easily and without fuss and guide you through the task using a highly visual, step-by-step approach – providing exactly what you need to know when you need it!

*Brilliant* guides provide the quick easy-to-access information that you need, using a detailed index and troubleshooting guide to help you find exactly what you need to know, and then presenting each task in a visual manner. Numbered steps guide you through each task or problem, using numerous screenshots to illustrate each step. Added features include 'See also...' boxes that point you to related tasks and information in the book, while 'Did you know?...' sections alert you to relevant expert tips, tricks and advice to further expand your skills and knowledge.

In addition to covering all major office PC applications, and related computing subjects, the *Brilliant* series also contains titles that will help you in every aspect of your working life, such as writing the perfect CV, answering the toughest interview questions and moving on in your career.

*Brilliant* guides are the light at the end of the tunnel when you are faced with any minor or major task.

## Publisher's acknowledgements

The author and publisher would like to thank the following for permission to reproduce the material in this book:

Mozilla Corp., FastMail Pty. Ltd., CyberLink Corp., Nullsoft Inc., WinZip International LLC., Live365 Inc., VLCPlayer.com, Zone Labs LLC., Lavasoft, GRISOFT s.r.o., CNET download.com, Fresh Communications Ltd., More2 Ltd, Advanced Micro Devices Inc., Kingston, Creative Technology Ltd, Plextor Corp. and Emma Cake.

Microsoft product screen shot(s) reprinted with permission from Microsoft Corporation.

Every effort has been made to obtain necessary permission with reference to copyright material. The publisher apologises if, inadvertently, any sources remain unacknowledged and will be glad to make the necessary arrangements at the earliest opportunity.

## Author's acknowledgements

The author would like to thank Paul Lester and Angela Kewley for equipment loan and proof-reading, and Sally and Karen at Syllaba for all their assistance.

## Dedication

To JD and JB.

## About the author

Matt Powell is a technical editor at Highbury Entertainment. He's written for a wide variety of computing magazines including *GigaHz*, *PC Home*, *Internet User*, *PC Basics*, *eBuyer*, *Windows XP Made Easy*, *PDA Essentials*, *Digital Photography Made Easy* and *PC First Aid*.

# Contents

# 3. Security and privacy                                       47

# Introduction

Welcome to *Brilliant Computer Basics*, a visual quick reference book that gives you a basic grounding in the way computers work, introduces the Windows operating system and demonstrates how to use common applications – a complete reference for the beginner user.

## Find what you need to know – when you need it

You don't have to read this book in any particular order. We've designed the book so that you can jump in, get the information you need, and jump out. To find the information that you need, just look up the task in the table of contents, index, or Troubleshooting guide, and turn to the page listed. Read the task introduction, follow the step-by-step instructions along with the illustration, and you're done.

## How this book works

Each task is presented with step-by-step instructions in one column and screen illustrations in the other. This arrangement lets you focus on a single task without having to turn the pages too often.

# Step-by-step instructions

This book provides concise step-by-step instructions that show you how to accomplish a task. Each set of instructions includes illustrations that directly correspond to the easy-to-read steps. Eye-catching text features provide additional helpful information in bite-sized chunks to help you work more efficiently or to teach you more in-depth information. The 'For your information' feature provides tips and techniques to help you work smarter, while the 'See also' cross-references lead you to other parts of the book containing related information about the task. Essential information is highlighted in 'Important' boxes that will ensure you don't miss any vital suggestions and advice.

# Troubleshooting guide

This book offers quick and easy ways to diagnose and solve common problems that you might encounter using the Troubleshooting guide. The problems are grouped into categories that are presented alphabetically.

# Spelling

You will notice that we have used American spelling conventions throughout this book. We do regret having to do this in a book aimed at UK and Irish readers. However, nearly all the software that we illustrate (Microsoft's being the most prevalent) is written by American developers and in order to be consistent with the spelling you will actually encounter whilst using your PC, we have conformed. Please rest assured that our grammatical conscience struggles as much as yours does with disk, color and program!

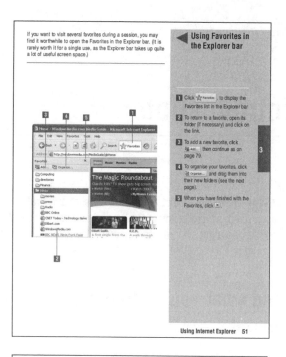

# Introducing your PC

## Introduction

Before we focus on software applications and how to actually use your computer to accomplish things, we're going to take a peek inside a PC to diskover what exactly it is each part does. Although this may be the last thing you want to do right now, a little knowledge about the innards of your computer can go a long way once you've mastered the operating system and software applications. Many minor problems can be fixed with a little hardware maintenance and all it'll take will be a screwdriver and perhaps a touch of elbow grease. There's absolutely no soldering, welding or hardware engineering involved! It can be a little scary the first time you pop open the case and see bundles of wires and mysterious slabs of silicon, but today's systems are modular and designed to be as simple as possible. Unless you ignore a few basic safety rules, it's very difficult to hurt either yourself or your PC. The most important of these is a no-brainer: always switch off the power to your system before opening the case. Shut the system down and then flick the power switch on the back of your power supply unit to ensure there's no chance it'll power up. You can safely leave it plugged in once the PSU is off and in fact this is recommended as it will keep your PC grounded. Static is the PC enthusiasts worst enemy and will fry the most delicate (and expensive) parts in the blink of an eye. Try not to perform maintenance while standing on carpet or any other material that easily builds static and always touch a grounded metal object beforehand to diskharge any build-up. You can also buy anti-static wristbands for a few pounds from any good PC store – they clip onto a metal surface and keep static from building. Magnetism and electronics don't mix either, so make sure you have a screwdriver with non-magnetic head and don't slap fridge magnets onto the side of your case! If you're going to be regularly poking about inside computers it's not a bad idea to purchase a proper PC toolkit, which will usually contain a screwdriver with the correct heads, anti-static wristband and many other useful extras. The final important safety tip is to never apply excessive force to any component. If you're trying to remove something and it's not budging, take your time, check for well-hidden catches, levers or screws and carefully try to work it out. The last thing you want to do is damage your graphics card or motherboard because you forgot about the catch holding it in place on the expansion slot.

### Important

Always switch of the power to your system before opening the case.

# Motherboard

Think of the motherboard like your PCs central nervous system. Its job is to connect and manage each component, shuttling data to the correct location. Not all motherboards are the same and the type of hardware you can use is restricted by what will physically fit on the board and what is supported by the motherboard chipset.

Continuing the biological analogy, the central processing unit (usually referred to as the CPU or processor) is the brain of any system. It does the hard work of calculating all the data it's given by the motherboard. The power of a CPU is measured in Ghz (older CPUs under 1Ghz were measured in Mhz) but increasingly manufacturers are leaving off the Ghz speed in marketing materials as it becomes less important. Processors run extremely hot, requiring heatsinks and powerful fans to cool them.

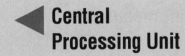

# Central Processing Unit

# RAM memory

Random Access Memory (RAM), or just memory, is extremely fast volatile memory that provides temporary data storage when a computer is in use. Volatile memory loses the data held when there's no power. The more RAM you have, the faster your system will operate as it's able to shunt data there while getting on with other tasks and retrieve it when needed. RAM often comes in pairs, but since there are many different kinds of RAM these must be of the same type and, preferably, from the same manufacturer.

The hard disk, hard drive or HDD is the main storage medium for modern computer systems. While RAM is volatile, hard disks are non-volatile so data written to them is kept until manually deleted. Current consumer level hard disks have reached 500 gigabytes (GB) in capacity. There are several types of interface for hard disks, the most common being IDE and SATA.

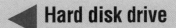 **Hard disk drive**

# Graphics card

The graphics card provides the vital function of processing and outputting visuals to your monitor. Some motherboards include graphics chips built onto to them but dedicated Graphics Processing Units (GPUs) offer hugely superior performance and save the CPU from having to handle graphics in addition to other tasks. Gamers demand expensive, high-end graphics cards but they're not necessary for standard Windows applications.

Sound cards provide audio capability to your system. Although most motherboards come fitted with adequate audio chipsets, musicians and gamers prefer dedicated sound cards as they usually offer better sound quality and a wider range of features.

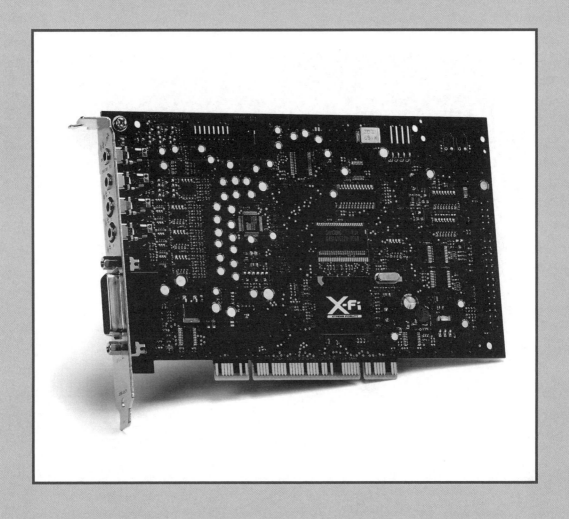

# Optical drive

Allows you to read and write CDs and DVDs. At bare minimum you'll need a DVD reader so you install software and play DVD video but writers, or burners, are now so cheap that there's little reason not to own one, especially since they offer such an easy and affordable backup solution.

The floppy drive, or FDD, has long since been superseded by CD and DVD drives but may still be useful to some who need to read old 3.5-inch floppy disks. They're so inexpensive that it makes sense to have one just in case.

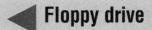 **Floppy drive**

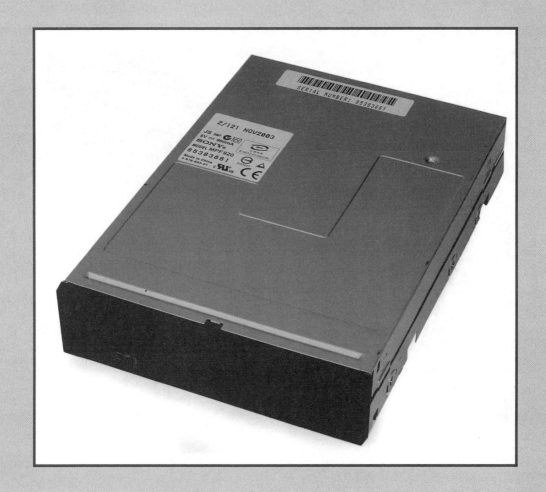

# Power Supply Unit

The Power Supply Unit (PSU) regulates and distributes power to your PC. Their output, measured in watts, is important as this limits how much hardware you can fit before your system's power requirements exceed the capability of the PSU. For most of us, a good quality 350W PSU is perfectly adequate.

Usually referred to as the case, enclosure, or chassis, this metal or plastic box is what holds all your components together. Cases vary in price and complexity from sub-£20 plastic models to high-tech aluminium costing many hundreds of pounds. If you have a choice it is worth looking at your options, since airflow, build quality and features can be important depending on your needs. If you're running a system with expensive high-end graphics cards and hard disks you'll need to ensure that there's a constant flow of cool air. You may also want extras such as tool-less operation, which allows you to open the case and remove components without a screwdriver, or accessible front-mounted interface ports.

◀ **PC case**

# Welcome to Windows

**2**

## Introduction

Microsoft's Windows XP, released in 2001, is the standard PC operating system. It's a massive improvement over previous incarnations offering a more user-friendly and stable computing platform (despite what some may have us believe.) If you're a newcomer to PCs though Windows can still be confusing, especially once you start delving into sub-menus and playing about with the myriad settings and options. In this opening chapter we're going to take you through the basics of the Windows operating system, kicking off with simple tasks like managing the desktop icons and customising the look and feel of your system. There are plenty of extra features included with Windows that make using it a far more pleasant and pain-free experience, so it obviously helps to know about them in advance.

## What you'll do

**Move and arrange icons around the desktop**

**Use the Desktop Cleanup Wizard**

**Use the taskbar**

**Configure the taskbar**

**Use the Quick Launch**

**Use and customise the Start Menu**

**Create and use folders**

**Customise Windows**

**Learn about power saving options**

**Learn about accessibility options**

## Windows though time

In November 1983 Microsoft, makers of the MSDOS operating system, announced Microsoft Windows; an extension of the MSDOS system. Windows was Microsoft's first Graphical User Interface (GUI). The evolution of computers from text-based instruction systems to icon-based control had begun.

Windows through time

1990 Windows 3x

1993 Windows NT

1995 Windows 95

1996 Windows NT workstation

1998 Windows 98

2000 Windows me and Windows 2000

2001 Windows XP Home and Windows XP professional

2006 Windows Vista launch due October

# Moving and arranging icons around the desktop

We're going to start off with the basics – how to manage the icons on your desktop. Although your desktop will be empty initially, it's not going to be long before you've filled it with files and program shortcuts. Not only can it become difficult to find what you're looking for, but performance can be affected as Windows struggles to update all the **icon** graphics each time it loads. The occasional spot of housekeeping will also make your PC look far more organised, although Windows XP already features an option that does the cleaning for you but it can't be relied upon not to move essential program **shortcuts**.

## Move icons

**1** Click on an icon, hold the mouse button and drag it to where you want it to go.

**2** Groups of icons can be moved by clicking and holding on an empty part of the desktop and dragging a selection box over them. Release the mouse then click and hold on any one of the selected icons to move all of them.

### Jargon buster

**Icon** – graphical representation of a file or other object. They usually indicate what type of file the item is but can be customised by the user.

**Shortcut** – link to another location on your computer. If you want to run an application, they save you from navigating to the directory where that program is stored.

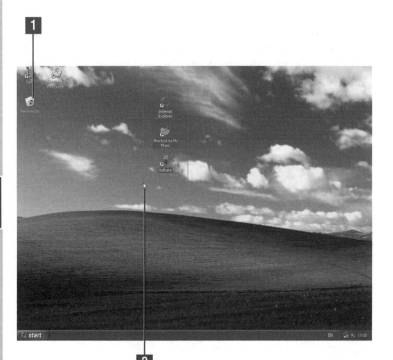

## Moving and arranging icons around the desktop (cont.)

### Arrange icons

**1** You can have Windows arrange icons by right-clicking on an empty part of the desktop to bring up the **context menu**, moving to Arrange Icons By and enabling Auto Arrange.

**2** You can choose the order in which they're arranged by selecting name, size, type or date modified in the menu.

**3** If you wish to place the icons anywhere on the desktop, disable both Auto Arrange and Snap To Grid options.

### Jargon buster

**Context menu** – the term given to the menu that appears when you right-click, so called because its functions change depending on the program or area of the operating system in which you currently reside.

### See also

Readers who have recently upgraded to WIndows XP from WIndows 98, 2000 or Me may prefer to use the Classic Start menu, which retains the same layout as the previous operating systems had. See page 23 to select this over the default.

# Using the Desktop Cleanup Wizard

▶

**1** Right-click on a blank area of the desktop, then click Properties, move to the Desktop tab and click Customize Desktop.

**2** Click Clean Desktop Now to run the cleanup Wizard. Clear the checkbox next to every icon you want to keep.

**3** Click Next to continue.

## Did you know?

Any icons on your computer can be moved and arranged in the same manner as desktop icons. Anywhere in Windows you can select icons and drag and drop to move them to different folders or locations, or arrange them using the context menu.

## Timesaver tip

You can use shortcut keys to grab icons. Hold down Shift then click once on the first and last icons in a group you want to select and they will all be highlighted. Holding Ctrl allows you to select one icon at a time, for example, choosing every other icon in a row. Combine these two by using Shift to select a group, releasing it, then selecting others or removing those already chosen by holding Ctrl and clicking once on any you don't want selected.

**1**

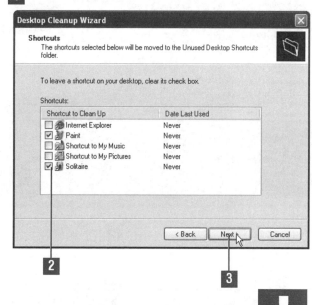

**2**

**3**

!

## Important

Windows will attempt to run the Desktop Cleanup Wizard every 60 days. If you don't want it to do this, remove the tick from the Cleanup Wizard checkbox in the Customize Desktop menu.

The taskbar is that grey bar that stretches the entire length of your screen with the Start Menu to the left and **system tray** to the right. When you open a program, it appears in the taskbar and can be minimized or bought back into focus by clicking once. Simple! You do have some additional options for customisation though, which can make it much easier to get access to your favourite applications and websites. Additional toolbars can be added or you can quickly rearrange program windows and **folders** for easy viewing.

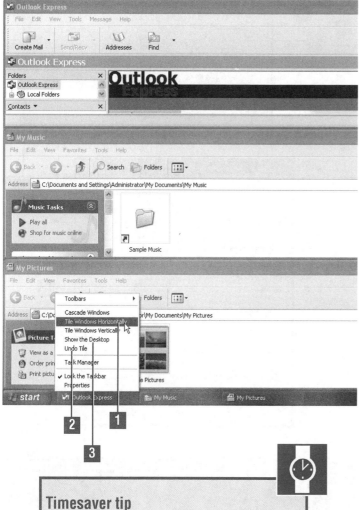

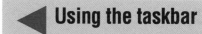

## Using the taskbar

2

### Arrange program and folder windows

**1** Right click on an empty section of the taskbar and choose Cascade or Tile from the context menu to align the visible windows automatically .

**2** Use Undo to reverse the window alignment you just set.

**3** Click Show the Desktop to minimize all windows and reveal the desktop.

### Jargon buster

**Folders** – also called directories, are what Windows uses to organise all the files. Think of them like the filing cabinets in an office, a way of keeping relevant files grouped together for easy access.

**System tray** – the area to the far right of the taskbar. It is often used by applications to display status icons, while some programs have the option to minimize to the system tray rather than the taskbar.

**Toolbars** – groups of related options and tools, usually represented by icons. Toolbars can be floating in a program window or embedded into the top or side of an application window (sometimes called sidebars.) Sidebars are often customisable, giving users the option to disable them or add and remove icons.

## Timesaver tip

Hold Alt and press Tab to bring up a menu that allows you to quickly switch between the programs on the taskbar. Keep tapping Tab until the program or window you want is selected then release both keys to bring it into focus.

# Configuring the taskbar

You can configure the taskbar through its Properties dialog box. To open this, right-click on the taskbar and choose Properties.

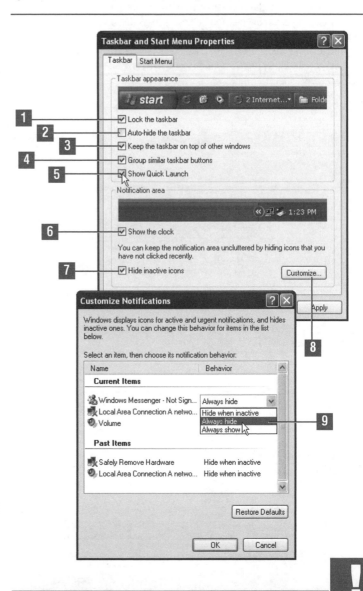

**1** Lock and unlock the taskbar with the Lock the Taskbar setting.

**2** Auto-hide will cause the taskbar to slide out of view until you place the mouse cursor over it.

**3** Disabling the option to keep the taskbar on top of other windows will hide it behind the current active folder or application.

**4** With Group Similar Taskbar Buttons enabled, buttons from the same application will be grouped when the taskbar is full.

**5** Enabling Quick Launch places a row of useful shortcut icons to the left of the taskbar.

**6** Disabling Show the Clock will remove the clock from the system tray

**7** Hide Inactive Icons is enabled by default and hides all system tray icons except those used recently.

**8** To set which icons will be hidden, choose 'Customize' next to the Inactive Tray Icons option.

**9** Hold the cursor over the behaviour setting for the icon you want to configure and choose an option from the drop-down box.

## Important

Many programs place icons in the System Tray. Some are there when Windows starts, others when a program is run. They can provide useful shortcuts to functions, but may not be essential to the operation of a program. Also, having too many running in the System Tray when Windows starts can slow down your PC. If you wish to disable System Tray icons, check the options and settings for applications that use it as they will usually allow you to remove them.

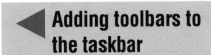

2

**1** You can enable a pre-defined toolbar by right-clicking on the taskbar, opening the Toolbars menu and clicking one of those already listed.

**2** Add your own by choosing New Toolbar from the toolbars menu. Select any folder on your system.

**3** You can also add websites by typing a web address into the Folder box.

**4** Remove custom toolbars by going back to the Toolbars menu and clicking on the unwanted toolbar.

**2**

New Toolbar  [?] [X]

Choose a folder, or type an Internet address

⊞ 📁 My Documents
⊟ 🖥 My Computer
  ⊞ 💾 3½ Floppy (A:)
  ⊞ 💿 Local Disk (C:)
  ⊞ 💿 WXPVOL_EN (D:)
  ⊞ 📂 Control Panel
  ⊞ 📁 Shared Documents
  ⊞ 📁 Administrator's Documents

**3**

Folder: My Computer

[Make New Folder]  [OK]  [Cancel]

### Timesaver tip

Folders can also be dragged onto the taskbar to instantly make them into toolbars.

**!**

### Important

On a fresh installation of Windows the language bar, which allows you to quickly switch languages, is enabled by default and placed to the right of the taskbar. You can disable this by right-clicking it and choosing Close. Take note of the message that appears telling you how to re-enable it via the Regional and Language Options settings.

# Using the Start Menu

The Windows Start Menu is where all your program shortcuts are stored; it allows you to get quick access to any installed applications (provided they've placed an icon there) plus various other tools like Search and **Control Panel**. It's also where you go to shut down, log-off or restart your computer, just don't question why the button you click to quit is labelled 'Start'! The Start Menu is easy to manage as it's simply a folder on your PC that contains all the shortcuts, so you can drag and drop icons to it like you would any other folder.

Name and icon of the current user – does not appear when using Classic Start Menu

Quick access to system folders, can be removed using the advanced menu in Start Menu properties – not visible in Classic mode

These can be customised via the Start Menu properties – not visible with Classic Start Menu

Shortcuts to frequently accessed applications – appear at the top of the menu when using Classic mode

Shortcuts to your applications – most programs should place icons here automatically, if not you can create your own

Opens a sub-menu or a new window – set the option in Start Menu properties. If set to sub-menu, double-click on the Control Panel icon to open it as a window.

Open the help wizard

Search your PC for files and folders

Command line prompt where you can run applications, files or web sites – useful if you need to add a command when running a program

Go back to the user logon screen

Power down the system

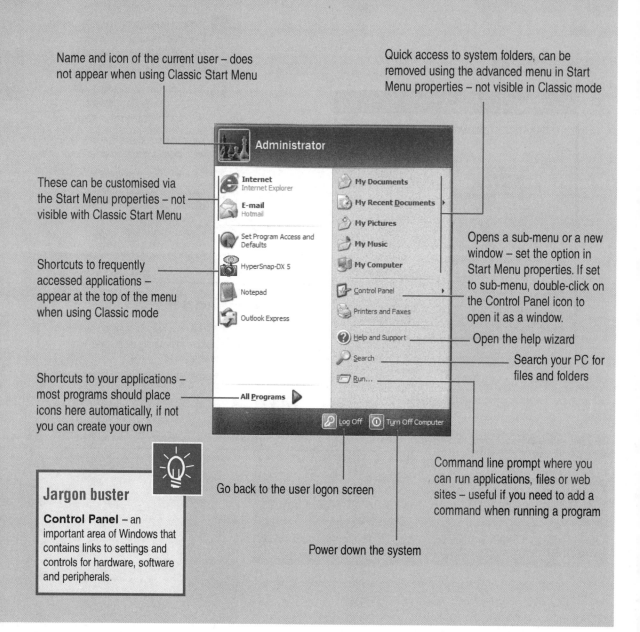

20

Quick Launch is a customisable shortcut bar that's enabled through the Start Menu properties. Applications will often place a shortcut here as well as on the desktop.

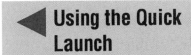

# Using the Quick Launch

**1** Click and drag icons onto the **Quick Launch** to make shortcuts. You can choose where the icon is placed before releasing the mouse button.

**2** Move icons on Quick Launch by dragging and moving them to a different position.

**3** Once you've filled up the space available to Quick Launch icons will be moved to a pop-up window, click the arrow to access them.

**4** Use the Show Desktop icon to instantly minimize every program and reveal the desktop.

**5** To increase the size of Quick Launch, unlock the taskbar by right-clicking on the taskbar and selecting Unlock, a bar will appear next to Quick Launch allowing you to extend its size.

## Important

With the Classic Start Menu enabled, you can immediately identify whether you're using Windows XP Home or Professional, as it will be labelled down the side.

# Customising the Start Menu

As with the rest of Windows, the Start Menu is customisable and has bundles of options to play with. You have a choice of sticking with the default Start Menu or switching to the slimmed-down Classic Start Menu, which is essentially the same as that found in Windows 98, 2000 or ME. Apart from the placement of shortcut icons and a few extra options there's little between them so it comes down to personal preference.

**1** You can move icons around on the Start Menu simply by clicking and dragging them to a new position, though it's much easier to organise by right-clicking on the Start button.

**2** You can choose Explore, Open or Explore All users from the Start Menu context options. Explore is the easiest to use if you're moving icons.

**3** Because the Start Menu is just another folder on your system, it works like any other directory within Windows. Grab folders or icons and drag them, or right-click to create a new folder.

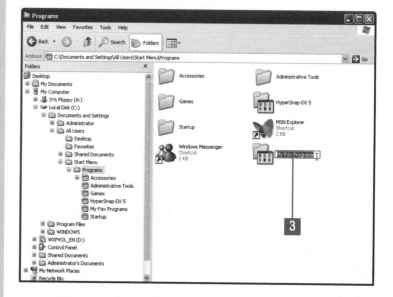

## Timesaver tip

If you want to create a shortcut to a file or folder, hold down the right mouse button when you drag an icon instead of the left. When you release it, a menu will appear asking if you want to Copy, Move or Create a Shortcut. This is very helpful when you want to move instead of copying and vice versa, or create shortcuts in the Start Menu or another location. Simply find the item you want to link, click and drag with the right mouse button and choose Create a Shortcut. If you hold the button while dragging and hover over the Start Menu or a minimized window in the taskbar for a second, it will open as though you had clicked on it. You can do this through subfolders in the Start Menu, releasing the button when you reach the desired location for the shortcut.

When setting Start Menu properties, the most important choice is that between Start Menu and Classic Start Menu. The former is default and has more options; the latter is cleaner and moves many icons, like My Computer, to the desktop.

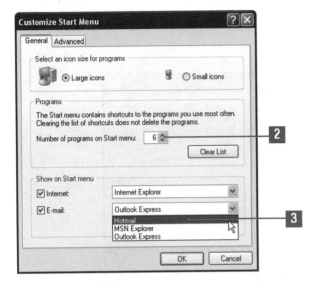

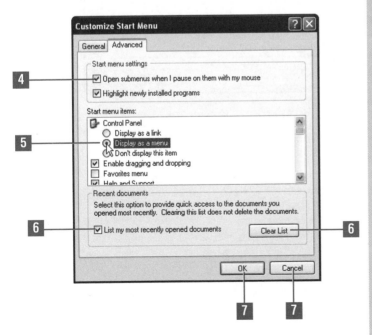

**1** Right-click on Start and choose Properties. Select Start Menu or Classic Start Menu, then click the Customize button next to the Start Menu option.

**2** Set how many recently used applications to list in the Start Menu.

**3** Disable the checkboxes to remove Internet and Email links, or choose alternative links. If you have a Hotmail account you can change the email link to take you straight to Hotmail.

**4** On the Advanced tab, if you disable the Open submenus option, menus will only appear when you click the left mouse button.

**5** The Start Menu Items options allow you to disable shortcuts to My Computer, My Documents and other folders or change the way in which the Start Menu behaves.

**6** The Recent Documents menu keeps track of recently opened files. Clear the list with the button or disable this function by clicking the checkbox.

**7** Click OK or Cancel to exit Start Menu Customize and choose Classic Start Menu then Customize.

# Using Start Menu properties (cont.)

## Customize the Classic Start Menu

**8** Click Add or Remove to manage Start Menu shortcuts through a wizard. The Advanced button opens up an Explorer window while Sort arranges icons into alphabetical order.

**9** The advanced options let you expand the Control Panel and other folders off the Start Menu so you don't need to open them to access a particular file or application.

### Important

Each user account has its own Start Menu configuration. If you wish to have a program available to every user on the system, make sure there is a shortcut in the 'All Users' Start Menu folder. For more information on user accounts, see Chapter 3.

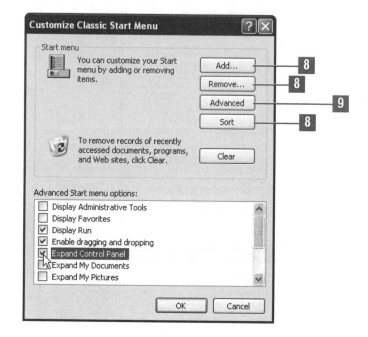

In Windows XP folders (or directories, if you like) offer plenty of options for customisation. Some of these are simply aesthetic changes that add sidebars and change the way icons are displayed, which you may or may not want depending on individual tastes, others are more functional such as the settings for hiding system files. Because Windows is integrated with Internet Explorer, folder windows are actually Internet Explorer windows and as such you can instantly navigate to a website from within them.

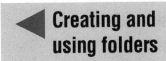

## Creating and using folders

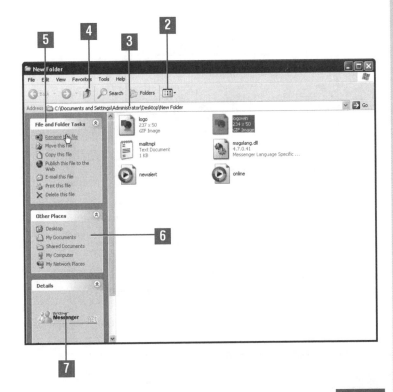

**1** Create a new folder by bringing up the context menu and choosing New folder, then entering a name. Folders can be created anywhere on your system.

**2** You can change the way icons are displayed by clicking the Views button and choosing a new layout.

**3** Type addresses (either local folders and hard disks or websites) into the Address Bar to navigate to them in the current folder window.

**4** Click the Up button to go up one folder in the directory tree.

**5** Use the File and Folder tasks sidebar to access common functions.

**6** The Other Places sidebar is like a favourites bookmark for locations on your hard drive, click these links to go directly to other system folders.

**7** The Details window gives information about the currently selected file and shows a preview if the file is an image or movie.

### See also

See Chapter 3 for details on Windows updates.

### Important

While you're able to install new web browsers and use them instead of Internet Explorer, it's unfortunately impossible to completely remove it from your system as Windows is so dependant on its presence. Because Internet Explorer represents such a high security risk, it's highly recommended that you keep Windows up-to-date with the latest program and security patches.

# Changing folder options ▶

1. When you're in a folder, click Tools then Folder Options.

2. Switch to Windows Classic folders to disable the Common Tasks sidebar.

3. Set the Browse Folders option to view folders in the existing window or open them in a new window.

4. The Click icons option allows you to make icons behave like web links, so a single click will open them. This applies to all icons on your system.

5. In the View tab, click Apply to all Folders to make the settings for the current folder universal.

6. By default, Windows hides system files and folders. In Advanced Settings, you can make these visible. There are also other settings that change the way files are displayed.

7. The File Types tab lists every known file on your system. Click New to manually add a **file extension**.

8. If you wish to change a file association so it opens with another program, select it in the registered file types list and click Change.

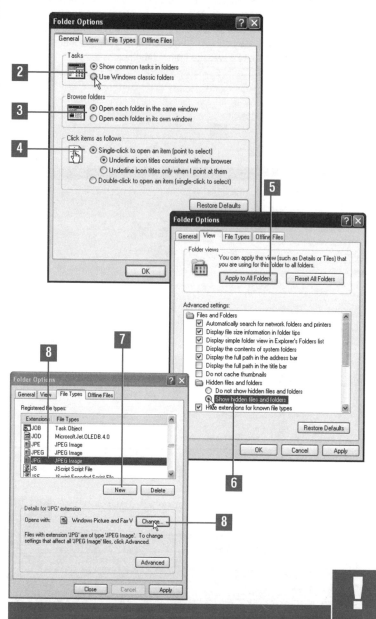

## Jargon buster

**File extension** – indicates the type of file. The response when the file is opened depends upon the application with which it is associated. Windows will prompt the user to select an action when unrecognised files are accessed.

## Important

Most applications will attempt to register themselves to handle certain file types when they're installed. If you install a new video player, for example, and don't want it to take over playing video files, make sure you check the installation options. Good programs ask before changing your file associations.

Since Windows 95, Microsoft's operating system has offered a wide range of features for customising the look and feel of the OS to suit the individual needs of each user, whether you want to change the way it behaves or simply use an attractive desktop background. The Windows XP Themes system allows you to quickly apply a universal theme to your PC, with matching background, icons, colors and sounds. There are also various settings for changing the general appearance and applying effects. If you have an older system, switching off the effects can make Windows feel noticeably snappier. It's not just about aesthetics, though. There are a number of accessibility features that can assist those with disabilities. For the hard of hearing or partially sighted these extra options can prove a godsend.

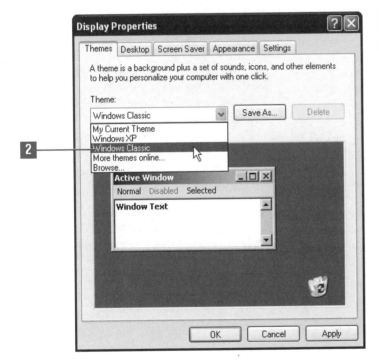

### See also
Go to page 41 to learn how to configure the built-in accessibility options.

# Selecting a desktop theme

**1** Right-click on a blank part of the desktop and choose Properties from the context menu.

**2** The Themes tab allows you to manage Windows XP themes. The default is 'Windows XP' but you can also select Windows Classic, which makes XP look like older versions of Windows.

### Important

Themes for Windows XP can be freely downloaded from various websites, Microsoft even provides some on its home page, in the Windows XP downloads section. Backgrounds are also widely available on thousands of websites, which can be found using any search engine. You can even create your own by making an image with the same dimensions as your desktop resolution.

# Choosing a desktop ▶ background

**1** The Desktop tab is where you select backgrounds. Choose an image from the list then click Apply.

**2** Click Browse to choose a new image from your computer.

**3** Use the Position options to select how the background will be displayed.

**4** The color settings change the color of the desktop behind the image. This will only be visible when there is no image selected or the image is centred, leaving a border.

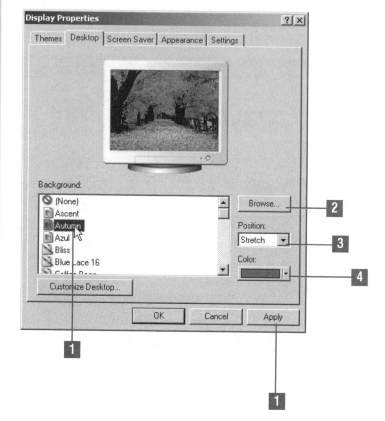

## Important

Desktop backgrounds look their best when their size matches the resolution of your desktop. If they're too small, the image will be stretched or centred with a border, too large and they'll be distorted.

28

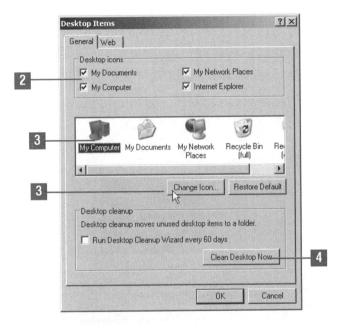

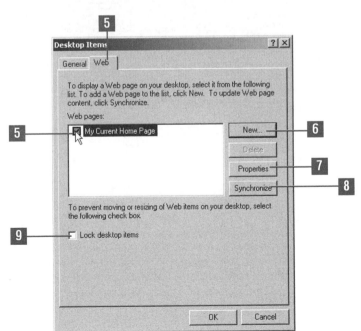

**1** Click the Customize Desktop button on the Desktop tab.

**2** Click the checkboxes to remove system icons from the desktop.

**3** Select an icon and click Change Icon to choose another icon graphic.

**4** Use the desktop cleanup wizard to remove unused icons. This will run every 60 days unless disabled.

**5** Click the Web tab. These options allow you to have a website as a background. Click the checkbox to set your current home page as the background.

**6** Click New to specify a site or locate an HTML file on your hard disk.

**7** Select a page from the list and click Properties to set schedules for synchronizing or choose options for downloads.

**8** Click Synchronize to download the latest version of the selected page.

**9** Enable the Lock Desktop option to stop web backgrounds being moved or resized.

# Choosing a screen saver

1. Click the Screen Saver tab.

2. Choose a new screen saver from the drop-down list.

3. Set a time for the delay between last activity and the screen saver enabling.

4. Enable the password option to password-protect your screen saver. The password will be the same as your Windows login. Note that in Windows XP Home edition, this option instead takes you back to the user logon screen.

5. Click Settings to change options for the current screen saver. These change depending on the screen saver.

6. Use Preview to check the screen saver.

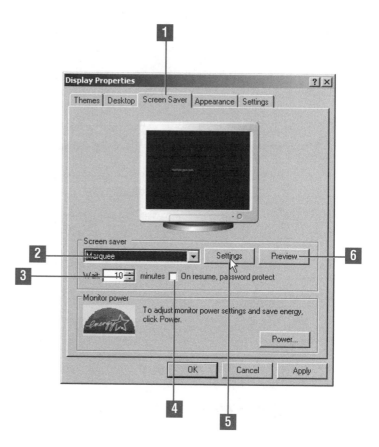

The Appearance tab gives you a greater amount of control over the look of Windows than you get from applying a Theme.

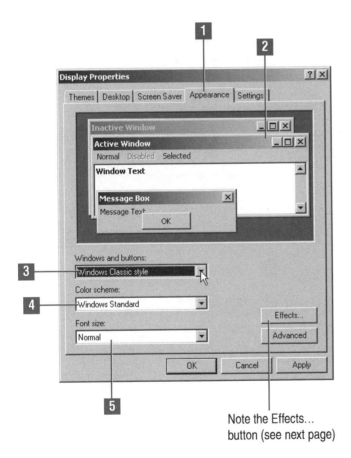

Note the Effects...
button (see next page)

**1** Click on the Appearance tab.

**2** This preview window shows you the effects of the changes you make, saving you from applying them to the whole desktop.

**3** Change the button and window style.

**4** Select a color scheme. A large number of pre-configured color schemes are already included.

**5** In the Font size area, choose Normal, Large and Extra Large.

# Setting additional options

**1** On the Appearance tab, click Effects for additional appearance options.

**2** The transition effects change the way in which menus appear, scrolling or fading into view. They can seem sluggish on older systems, so you may want to disable this option.

**3** Font smoothing removes the jagged edges from text. ClearType font smoothing is specifically designed for flat-panel displays and it does make text appear noticeably clearer.

**4** Enable large icons. This can be useful for those with impaired vision.

**5** Enable or disable drop-shadows on menus.

**6** By default, window contents are shown when dragging. Disable this and it will show an outline of the window instead.

**7** This option enables and disables the underlining of keyboard navigation shortcut keys, which are used to access the menus in applications using just the keyboard.

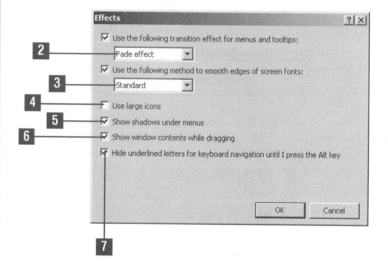

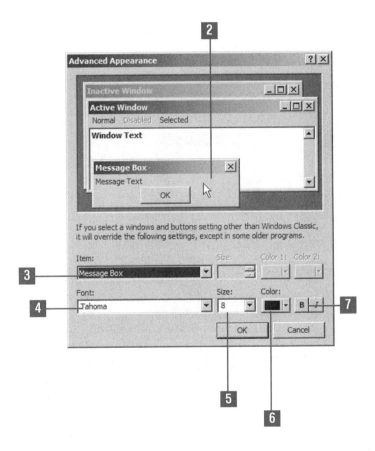

## Creating a custom color set

**1** Back in the Appearance tab – click Advanced. These options allow you greater control over colors and fonts.

**2** Use the preview window to not only see the effects of your changes, but also select which areas you want to edit by clicking them in the preview. The selected area will then appear in the Item box.

**3** Use the Item box to select the part of Windows that you want to customise.

**4** When applicable, the font box allows you to choose an alternative font for various window elements.

**5** Use the size options to adjust the size of window elements and fonts.

**6** Select a color for the windows and text. Click Other in the color pop-up box to create a custom color.

**7** Choose between bold and italic text styles. Click the current selection to remove all styling.

## Setting a resolution and color quality

The resolution defines the clarity of an image. With monitors, it describes the number of pixels on screen, so a 1280x1024 resolution means that there are 1024 lines of 1280, a total of 1,310,720 pixels. The maximum resolution changes depending on the capabilities of the monitor. All new 17–19" LCD monitors are capable of anything up to 1280x1024, with larger monitors handling 1600x1200 and varying specifications for widescreen displays.

**1** Monitor and graphics card options are found under the Settings tab in Display properties.

**2** Use the slider to change resolution. Do not take this over the maximum resolution for your monitor.

**3** The color quality should always be 32-bit. Only old systems will be incapable of handling 32-bit color. Time to upgrade if yours can't handle it!

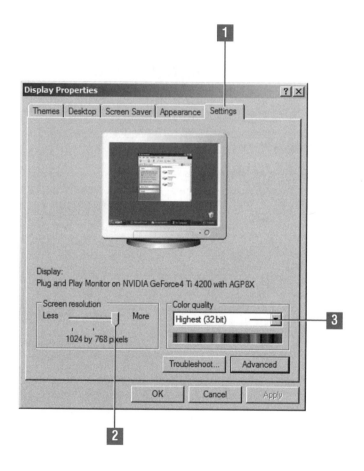

## Changing Windows sound effects

**Sounds and Audio Devices Properties**   ? ×

| Volume | Sounds | Audio | Voice | Hardware |

A sound scheme is a set of sounds applied to events in Windows and programs. You can select an existing scheme or save one you have modified.

Sound scheme:

Windows Default

Save As...    Delete

To change sounds, click a program event in the following list and then select a sound to apply. You can save the changes as a new sound scheme.

Program events:

- Windows
  - Asterisk
  - Close program
  - Critical Battery Alarm
  - Critical Stop
  - Default Beep

Sounds:

Windows XP Restore    ▶   Browse...

OK    Cancel    Apply

2

**1** Open Control Panel by either going to Start then Control Panel or Start, Settings, Control Panel. Once there, open Sounds and Audio Devices and click the Sounds tab.

**2** Two sound schemes are included – Windows Default and No Sounds. Select one from the list and it'll ask if you want to save the previous scheme.

**3** To customise the sounds, choose an event from the Program Events list and then select a sound from the list.

**4** You can use any WAV audio file on your computer, just click Browse and locate the file you wish to use. Press the Play button to preview the sound.

**5** Click Save As once you've configured your custom sound profile and give it a name. It'll then be added to the Sound Scheme drop-down list.

# Adjusting Power Settings

To help you conserve energy, keep the electric bills down and extend the life of your computer, there is a number of power saving features built into Windows XP. Using either a pre-defined power scheme or custom settings you can control how your system behaves when there is a period of inactivity. For laptops, Windows can even monitor the state of the battery and warn you when it runs low. There is also a hibernation feature that shuts down your PC, saving current programs, and restores them when you start the system.

**1** Power Options are accessible either through the Control Panel or from the Screen Saver tab of the Display Properties dialog.

**2** Use the Power Schemes tab to customise the behaviour of your system. You can select how long the computer will wait from the last activity before shutting down part or all of the system. Laptops will have an additional 'Running on Batteries' option.

**3** Choose a time limit or disable the power function by choosing Never from the drop-down list.

**4** Click Save As to store your current Power Scheme.

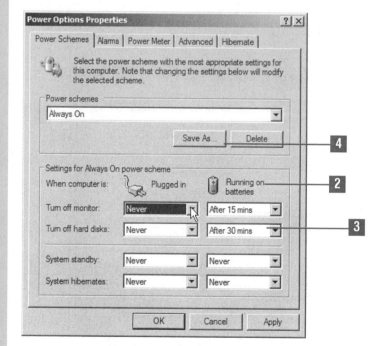

On portable systems, the Power Options Properties dialog box also includes an Alarms tab.

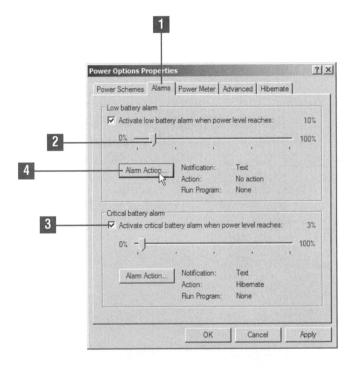

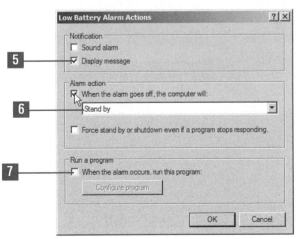

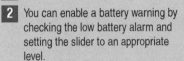
**1** Switch to the Alarms tab.

**2** You can enable a battery warning by checking the low battery alarm and setting the slider to an appropriate level.

**3** The critical alarm is a secondary option that warns you when the battery is extremely close to running out of juice.

**4** Click Alarm Action to configure the response to a low battery alarm.

**5** Set a notification, either a sound alarm or a message.

**6** You can force the system to shut down or enter hibernation when the alarm is triggered by enabling the Alarm Action function.

**7** It is also possible to run a program when the alarm goes off. Check this option then click configure program to select the application.

# Monitoring
# battery life

The Power Meter is another option only available for battery-powered portable systems.

**1** Switch to the Power Meter tab.

**2** Disable the Show Details for Each Battery option to see the total available power.

**3** Click the battery icon to see further details about a battery.

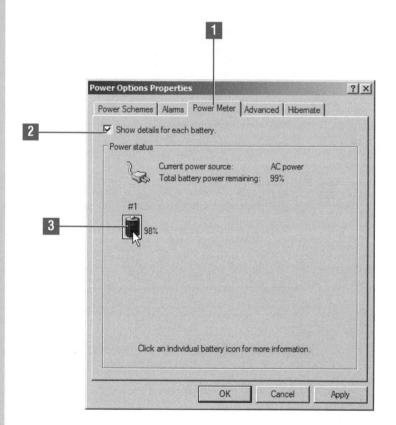

## Configuring Advanced Power Settings

**Power Options Properties**

Power Schemes | Alarms | Power Meter | **Advanced** | Hibernate

Select the power-saving settings you want to use.

**Options**

☐ Always show icon on the taskbar

☑ Prompt for password when computer resumes from standby

**Power buttons**

When I close the lid of my portable computer:

[Stand by ▼]

When I press the power button on my computer:

[Shut down ▼]

When I press the sleep button on my computer:

[Stand by ▼]

[ OK ] [ Cancel ] [ Apply ]

**1** Click the Advanced tab.

**2** Check the Show Icon on the taskbar to be able to quickly access your power options. This will only be useful if you regularly swap profiles or are using a battery-powered portable system and need to monitor the state of the batteries.

**3** Enable Prompt for Password to have the system ask for your login password when it resumes. This is a useful security feature if you're on a shared system.

**4** You can set how your system will behave when you press the power and reset buttons or, if you're on a laptop, shut the lid. If you do not have a dedicated sleep button, you may find it useful to have the computer enter hibernation whenever you press the power button.

### Timesaver tip

To get the most out of your laptop battery, don't forget to unplug external devices that may draw power like USB peripherals, whenever they're not in use. You should also leave your notebook hooked up to a wall and charging whenever possible to get the most out of the battery and if you're planning on going away for long periods, consider investing in a second battery as a backup.

### Important

For mission-critical systems an Uninterruptible Power Supply, or UPS, protects data in the event of a power failure by acting as a battery backup. Previously, a UPS would only be found on corporate servers and other important systems but simple UPS devices can now be purchased for the home user. While these do not have comparable features to a 'proper' UPS, they can act as a safety barrier when the electricity fails, giving you enough time to save your work and safely shut down the system. On desktop systems, Windows can detect a UPS device and monitor the power levels, the controls for which can be found in the Power options.

# Enabling hibernation mode

Hibernation shuts your computer down but saves its current state, including any open applications and windows. When your system starts up, it will boot quicker and all your previous windows will be restored.

**1** Click the Hibernate tab.

**2** Click Enable Hibernation to enable or disable hibernation mode.

**3** Hibernation mode needs to use the hard disk to store data. Ensure that you always leave enough free disk space before using Hibernation mode.

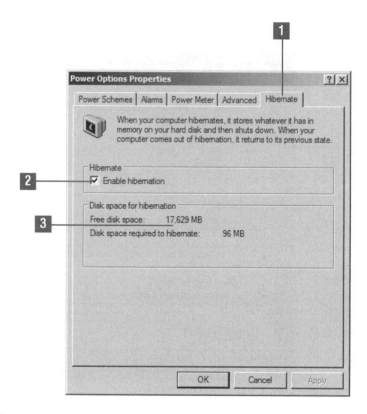

Included in Windows XP are tools to assist disabled and elderly users. If you are hard of hearing, partially sighted or have difficulty using a keyboard or mouse there's no need to miss out as the operating system can be easily customised to suit your needs. As you'll see, these are easy to use and may be helpful even if you don't have any special requirements that need addressing.

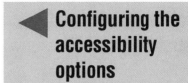

# Configuring the accessibility options

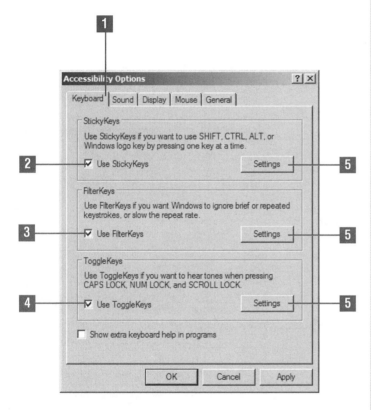

## Enable keyboard options

**1** Accessibility Options are found in the Control Panel. The first tab in this dialog screen, Keyboard, allows you to enable a number of useful widgets.

**2** Sticky Keys makes Ctrl, Alt, Shift and the Windows key behave like Caps Lock – you will only need to press these once to use them and once more to turn them off.

**3** Filter Keys will stop a key being repeated if it's held down or it can ignore repeated keystrokes.

**4** With Toggle Keys enabled you will hear a noise when Caps Lock, Num Lock and Scroll Lock are pressed.

**5** Use the Settings buttons to configure each individual feature and also view or disable the shortcut key needed to activate each feature.

# Enabling audio and visual helpers

**1** Click the Sound tab.

**2** SoundSentry will visibly alert you when the system makes a sound. You can choose the method it uses from the drop-down menu.

**3** ShowSounds will enable captions for any sounds generated in a program.

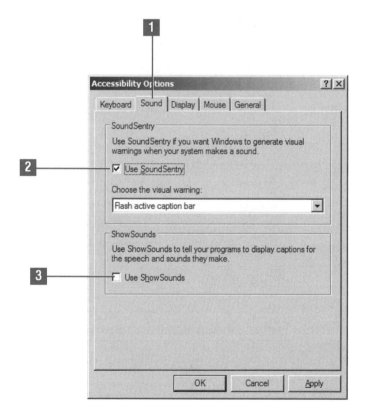

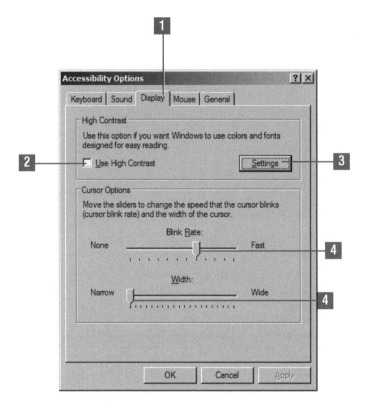

**1**

**Accessibility Options**                               ? X

Keyboard | Sound | Display | Mouse | General |

**2**

High Contrast
Use this option if you want Windows to use colors and fonts
designed for easy reading.

☐ Use High Contrast                    Settings          **3**

Cursor Options
Move the sliders to change the speed that the cursor blinks
(cursor blink rate) and the width of the cursor.

Blink Rate:

None  ———————▭————— Fast             **4**

Width:

Narrow ▭————————— Wide               **4**

OK          Cancel          Apply

**1** Open the Display tab.

**2** High Contrast uses color schemes
that make the desktop much easier to
use for the visually impaired. Click to
enable this is required.

**3** Click the Settings button to open a
dialog box with a large number of
color scheme options to choose from.

**4** You can set the cursor blink rate and
the size of the cursor using the sliders
to help make it easier to see.

2

# Enabling MouseKeys

MouseKeys allow you to use the cursor keys in place of the mouse. You can configure the speed and acceleration to suit yourself.

**1** Click the Mouse tab then check the box to enable control of the mouse with the cursor keys. Press settings to configure MouseKeys.

**2** Click Use Shortcut to run MouseKeys with a keyboard shortcut. Unfortunately you cannot select the shortcut keys yourself.

**3** Use these sliders to adjust the top speed and acceleration of the mouse pointer when controlling it with MouseKeys.

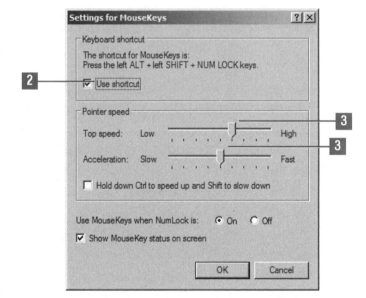

# Configuring general accessibility options

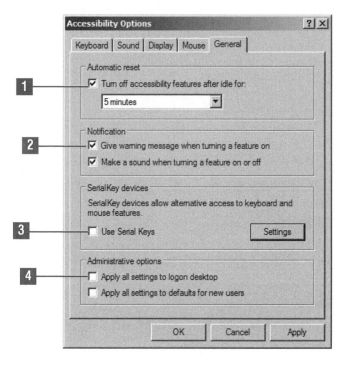

1. Accessibility features can be automatically switched off by enabling the auto reset. Choose a time limit from the drop-down list.

2. Select a notification method by enabling these settings.

3. Serial Keys is an option for specialised input devices to replace the keyboard and mouse. Select a COM port and baud rate in the Settings.

4. Use the Administrative options to apply the accessibility features to the logon screen and any new user profiles created.

## Timesaver tip

If the text on a website is too small to read, hold down Ctrl and spin the mouse wheel to zoom in and out. This also works in some other applications, such as word processors.

# Security and privacy

**3**

## Introduction

Security is a big buzzword in modern computing. Keeping the contents of your hard drive safe from the prying eyes of others is an uphill battle, and with the advent of **broadband** meaning more and more users are logging on every day, the risk of exposing your files and folders to the masses has increased exponentially over the last few years. Luckily, the 'good guys', security software vendors and Microsoft themselves have been working round the clock to stay ahead of the hackers, data-collectors and spies. Improvements to the Windows operating system, and a wide range of free or very reasonably priced security software, has actually made it easier than ever before to protect your machine. One of the biggest innovations of recent times has actually been made possible due to the success of broadband. Live updates are now common across not only antivirus software but firewalls and anti ad-ware and spy-ware tools, meaning that the latest definitions to defeat the latest security loopholes and viruses can be made available to you seconds after they are conceived. In this chapter we'll show you how to beef up security on your home PC, and we're focusing on ease of use as well, so even the least ambitious of beginners will have no trouble setting up a shield to beat away the malicious masses.

### Jargon buster

**Broadband** – traditionally the name given to a service which uses a single wire to carry many signals, for example cable telephone services that also provide television. Recently it has been applied to fast internet connections though ISPs will call anything from 256k upwards broadband when many don't believe that is true broadband as it's not fast enough. Most broadband connections now are at least 512k.

## What you'll do

**Secure Windows**

**Control services and processes**

**Use Windows Security Center**

**Control user access**

**Change logon and log-off settings**

**Protect your system from viruses**

**Download and install ZoneAlarm**

**Use your firewall**

**Protect your system from spyware**

**Scan for spyware**

**Protect your system with Ad-Watch and Process-Watch**

**Protect your system with passwords and encryption**

**Lock and encrypt files, folders and programs**

**Block websites**

**Use WinGuard's Extra Features**

# Securing Windows ▶

Before we even get onto installing firewalls and antivirus applications, there are a number of steps you should take to secure Windows. Microsoft provides an auto-update service at www.windowsupdate.com and it's absolutely vital that you visit this regularly to keep your system protected. Security holes are diskovered frequently and the Windows Update site will help safeguard your system by installing the latest security fixes. It's also a smart idea to learn how to monitor your system for changes. There are plenty of programs – both malicious and benign – that will attempt to place themselves in the system tray or load with Windows, so keeping an eye on what's going on in the background can help you minimize security risks as well as system clutter.

## Patch your system with Windows Update

**1** You'll need to use Internet Explorer for Windows Update. It does work with other browsers but you won't be able to take advantage of the auto-update functions, instead patches will have to be downloaded manually. Head over to www.windowsupdate.com to start.

**2** You may be prompted to download software for Windows Update itself – you must complete this to continue updating.

**3** Microsoft has recently introduced a validation program. Anyone wishing to install updates must have their operating system checked to ensure it's an officially licensed copy. If you do not pass the validation you will only be allowed to download critical security updates.

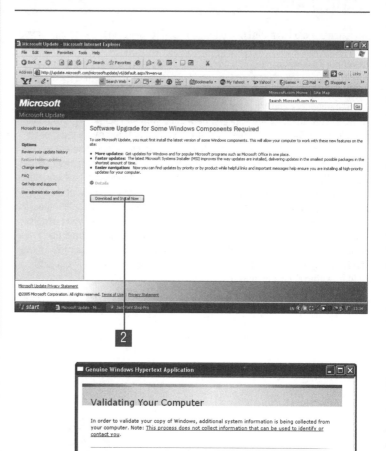

## Jargon buster

**Virus** – software program created for the purpose of causing damage to the system it infects. Some viruses simply damage files, others take over the systems and allow them to be remotely controlled, turning them into 'zombies'. This can be dangerous, as there have been cases where zombie systems were used to store pornography and pirated software without the knowledge of the owner.

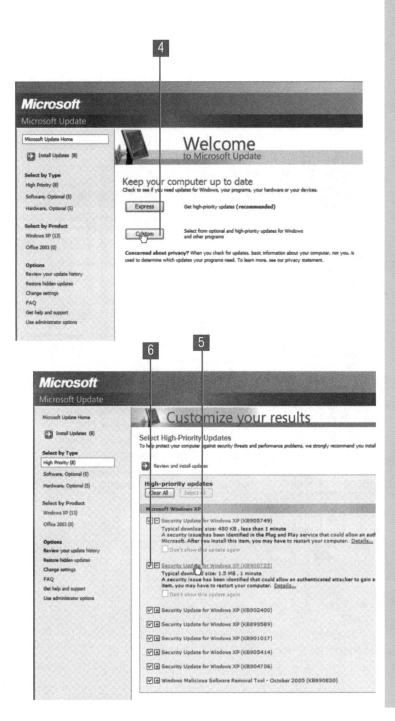

4 Choose either Express or Custom updates. Express will automatically select critical updates only, while Custom allows you to select which updates you download. We're going with Custom as it allows more control over the updates.

5 Click the update's name or the plus sign on its left to display more information about it.

6 Select which updates you wish to download by checking the box next to each entry. Click the plus and minus symbols to see more information about an update.

3

# Securing Windows (cont.) ▶

**7** Keep an eye on the information at the top, which tells you the total file size of your updates and an estimated download time.

**8** Choose the type of updates you wish to install. High priority are already selected by default, optional software and hardware updates will need to be manually added to the download queue.

**9** View previous updates you've downloaded with the Update History option.

**10** If you have chosen to hide certain updates previously, you can restore them by selecting the restore hidden updates option.

**11** At the Review and Install updates stage, click Install Updates to begin downloading the selected updates.

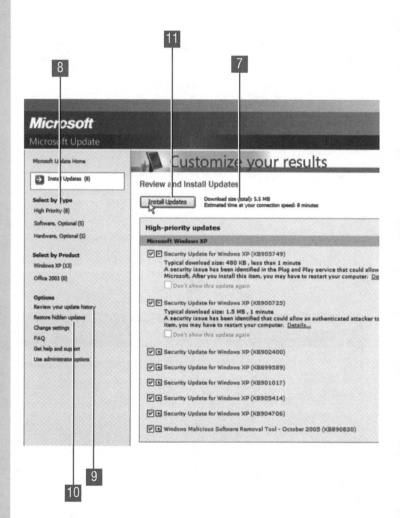

**12**

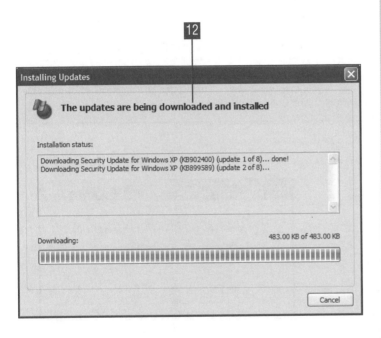

Installing Updates

The updates are being downloaded and installed

Installation status:

Downloading Security Update for Windows XP (KB902400) (update 1 of 8)... done!
Downloading Security Update for Windows XP (KB899589) (update 2 of 8)...

Downloading:                                    483.00 KB of 483.00 KB

Cancel

**12** Your updates will now be downloaded. Once all the files have been saved to your hard disk they will be automatically installed. The time taken will vary depending on the speed of your PC and internet connection. You may need to restart your system once this is complete.

3

## Important

Service Packs are occasionally released by Microsoft to introduce new features and update the operating system. The latest release for Windows XP is Service Pack 2 which, as well as patching many holes in the operating system, includes new security features to help protect against viruses and hackers. If you don't already have SP1 or SP2 installed, Windows Update will attempt to install them. We'd recommend that you do this if prompted because the packs include some important and useful extras.

# Controlling services and background processes

Whenever Windows starts up, it initialises a number of processes in order to get itself ready for you to use. These are programs that run invisibly in the background, and offer additional functionality or provide you with access to additional tools or accessibility features. Processes are often employed and started by applications you've installed to your hard drive, such as virus-checkers that keep running in the background to keep your system free from infection. If you've installed a lot of software for various reasons since you've had your machine, you might find you have an inordinate amount of these services and processes running, many of which may not actually be necessary for the day-to-day running of your computer. It must be stressed at this point that stopping services or processes that are vital to the running of Windows or its installed applications may cause problems and you may find programs cease to run. It's fairly easy to revert back to your original settings but you should take care when carrying out these sorts of changes to your operating system regardless. Successfully removing services or processes that aren't needed can not only improve the overall security of your system but speed up your machine as well. All of this can be accomplished by using the built-in Microsoft Configuration Tool.

## Open the Configuration Tool

**1** Click the Start menu and choose the Run command on the right.

**2** Type 'Msconfig' into the text box that appears and press return to load the Microsoft Configuration Tool.

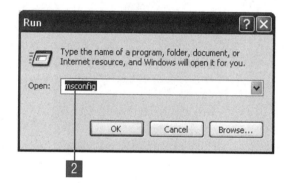

The startup options give you three choices for booting your system. By default, the selective startup is used, which uses system files set up with specific processes and services to load. You can choose to run a full boot, which loads everything on your system or a diagnostic startup to load basic drivers only. If you have problems starting your system or running applications after making changes, you can try booting with one of these alternative options.

**1** Select an appropriate startup option, if required.

**2** The Services tab is one way to change the services that load with Windows or to stop services that are currently running. An alternative method here is to use the Component Services tool, which we'll look at a bit later.

**3** The Startup tab shows the software that loads when your computer boots up, much of which may well be unnecessary. We'll show you how to prevent software or add-ons you don't really need from booting with Windows a bit later.

3

**4** System Restore is a Windows safeguarding tool that allows you to revert your operating system to a previous state. This is an excellent way to regain control of Windows if the changes you've made are making it unstable, since all of Windows' settings from this previous date are restored.

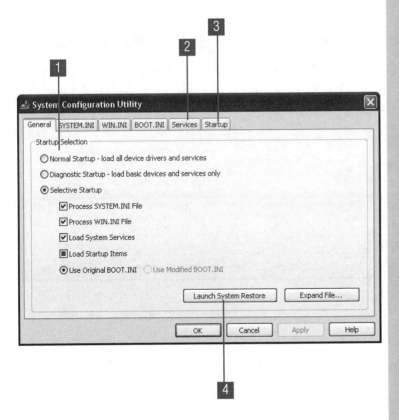

# Using MSConfig (cont.)

## Use the MSConfig Startup tab

**1** The left column in this list is the name of the startup item running on your computer. The name may now always make it obvious exactly what process this item is starting, so you'll need to use the other two columns here to help.

**2** The second column shows the command line of the process that is running. This is the command executable and any associated parameters used to start the process. The path in this string should give you a good idea of exactly which application is utilising this process.

**3** These two buttons are simply shortcuts to enabling or disabling all of the processes at once, and isn't usually recommended. You should pick and choose processes to stop or restart based on what you know from the filename and path of the process. Use the tickboxes alongside individual rows to control that particular process.

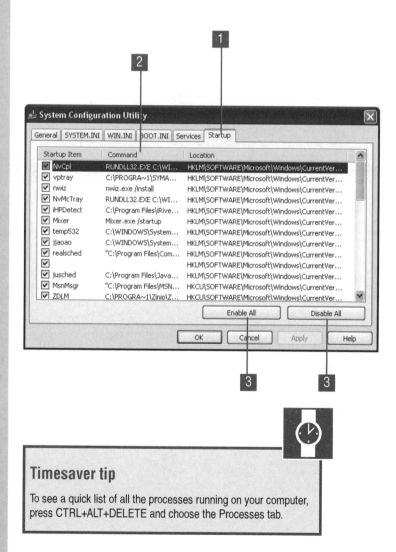

## Timesaver tip

To see a quick list of all the processes running on your computer, press CTRL+ALT+DELETE and choose the Processes tab.

Task Manager allows you to see and control what is happening on your system. The Processes tab shows all the processes that are running, and how much of the system's resources they are using.

1. Click the Processes tab to view the processes currently running on your computer.

2. Right-click a process to raise its priority with your operating system or more commonly to terminate if you suspect it is causing problems with your machine.

3

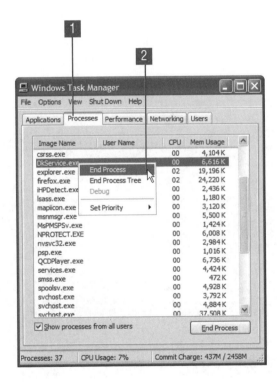

# Editing and configuring Windows Services

▶

Windows uses a myriad of services to control the day-to-day running of your PC and prepare itself for the various tasks you might want to complete during a session. For the most part, Windows itself is very poor at streamlining these services to cope with the tasks you use your computer for, and you may find there are services enabled and running that you really don't need. Streamlining services can both increase security and speed up your machine, so it's worth reading up a bit more about them in case you want to do this yourself. The best way to find out more about what each service does and what options you have for changing the default settings is to read up online. If you run a Google service for 'Windows Services' you should find a few results. We've used Black Viper's Windows XP webpage at www.blackviper.com/WinXP/servicecfg.htm. Browse to this or a similar site and you should see a list of common Windows services together with better explanations and your various options. We'll show you how to change your service settings once you've got the information you need on how they perform.

**1** The Black Viper homepage provides you with plenty of information on Windows services, and will tell you what settings to use for services depending on how you want to use your PC. Simply click the name of the service in their list to find out more.

**2** As a summary guide, the corresponding table shows the service settings for different categories of computer. Once you've familiarised yourself with each category you can scan through this table to check the service setting and change your services as you see fit.

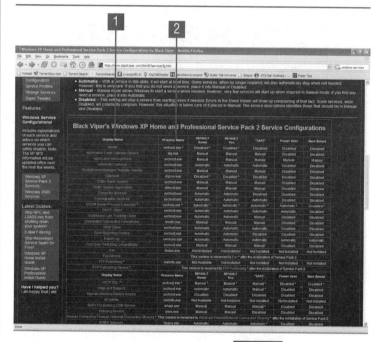

## Important

Stopping processes, and particularly changing service settings, are Windows tweaks that can cause problems if you're not sure what you're doing. If you do decide you want to streamline your machine by shutting down processes you deem unnecessary, it's not advisable to make widespread changes in one go. Instead of turning off eight processes and disabling twenty services in one go, for example, do two or three at a time and then reboot your machine. If you can perform all the usual operations and open applications without problems, change a few more and reboot again. This way if something does go wrong it'll be far easier to work out exactly what may be causing the problem.

The component services are a set of tools for modifying the setup of your PC. You need to be logged in as an Administrator to modify these settings.

## Accessing the Administrative tools

1. Open the Control Panel and double-click Administrative Tools, then double click Component Services.

2. Click the Services (Local) icon in the tree list on the left to open the services display.

3. The first column shows the name of the process, which may be referred to in errors, instructions or guides to manipulating your Windows environment as you delve deeper into modifying the setup of your PC.

4. The description column should give you some idea of exactly what the service does and perhaps how vital it is to the way you run your machine.

5. The status column informs you whether or not the process is currently started and running on your system.

6. The startup type column tells you how Windows treats the service on bootup. Some services are started automatically, others need to be manually started and others may be disabled altogether.

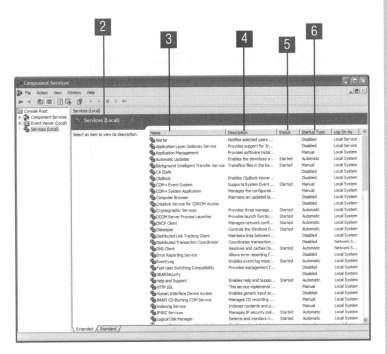

3

# Changing service settings

**1** To change services settings, right-click the service and choose Properties from the context menu.

**2** You'll find the name of the service and a description of how it affects your machine at the top of this window.

**3** The path to the executable file that runs the service, along with any parameters that are included is shown here.

**4** The startup type can be changed from this dropdown list. You can choose whether to automatically or manually start the service, or disable it altogether.

**5** If you change the settings for the service, they may not leave the desired results until the system is rebooted. To immediately start, stop, pause or resume a service without waiting for reboot use the command buttons shown here.

**6** Click the OK or Apply button to enforce any changes you've made, or the Cancel button to disregard them and revert to the service's original state.

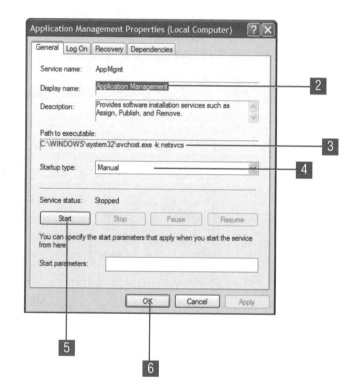

If you've installed the Windows Update tools and configured your machine to download the latest updates, including Service Pack 2, you may have noticed an addition to the Control Panel when you rebooted. The much needed Windows Security Center is intended to help you gauge and manage your current system security, and makes far more sense than trawling through a series of unrelated menus and windows to find the **firewall** settings, for example. Open the Security Center and you'll find it not only related to Microsoft's built-in security, but keeps track of third party security software you have installed on your system as well. Initially reassuring as a brief summary that you have the major levels of protection required, you can also find out more about each type of security and tweak and adjust the built-in Windows tools like the Windows Firewall.

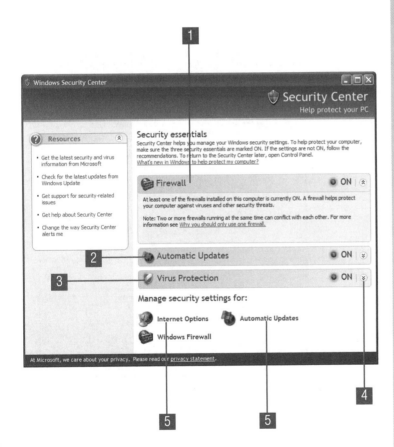

## Using Windows Security Center

1. The firewall settings let you know if either the Windows Firewall or a third party firewall is currently enabled on your operating system.

2. The automatic updates setting is important in order to receive the latest security updates and Windows enhancements. You should leave this on unless you find it seriously drains resources on your computer.

3. Virus protection is essential for any modern PC. If you have third-party antivirus software installed it will register here.

4. Click the double-arrows next to any of the items to expand it and read more about the important of this type of security.

5. To change security settings for your firewall, automatic updates or internet options, click one of the shortcut links at the bottom of this window.

### Jargon buster

**Firewall** – a barrier between the internet and your computer. It protects from outside threats like viruses and hackers by filtering the incoming data, blocking any potentially harmful information. Firewalls are an absolutely vital part of any system connected to the internet.

# Configuring the Windows Firewall ▶

Despite Service Pack 2's addition of a more user friendly Security Center, the firewall is no easier to use, and only advanced users will be comfortable adjusting the settings using the tools on offer. We'll show you how to install a more useful, friendly and far more configurable firewall a bit later in this chapter.

**1** We've selected the Windows Firewall link at the bottom of the Security Center window to check the status of this firewall. You can use the tabbed list along the top to view the current settings, open ports or add exceptions to your current firewall configuration.

**2** Click the On button to turn the firewall on if you don't already have one installed. If you're currently working without any firewall, you should turn on the Windows Firewall now, at least for the time being,

**3** If you have another firewall installed you can leave the Windows Firewall off by choosing the Off option.

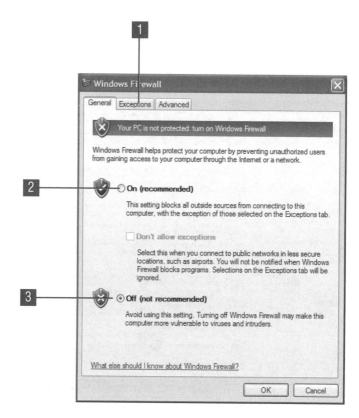

The ability to handle multiple users as standard was introduced into Windows XP to give families and those working from home or on shared machines a chance to have their own individual settings and access privileges. From a convenience point of view it's a great way to avoid arguments and keep your own personalised desktops and folder structure, but it also has a strong security benefit if you work on a shared machine. By setting up and using multiple accounts you can install different applications for each user and restrict access to critical parts of the operating system. Files and folders that you've created will only be visible to you, so when you log off you can be sure that the next user won't be able to access the files you've just created.

Whether or not you consider a shared machine to be a security risk, it's worth setting up user accounts so you can control user access anyway, and is very easy to do.

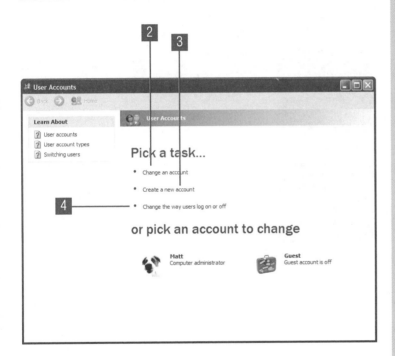

# Controlling user access

**1** Click the Start menu and choose the Control Panel, then double-click the User Accounts icon in Classic view.

**2** Change an account. Choose an account to change from those currently set up. You can adjust settings here such as name, password, picture and account type and access privileges. You'll need the password for the account you're changing if you're not logged in under it.

**3** Create a new account. Here you can add a new account for a new user on the system, and configure their privileges and settings. Once you've set up this new account it will be available from the user account list when Windows starts up.

**4** Change the way users log on or off. Here you can choose to have Windows show all the accounts when it starts so you can select the relevant one, or enable fast **user switching** so you can move quickly back and forth between active user accounts without losing any of your settings.

## Jargon buster

**User switching** – a Windows option that allows you to quickly switch from one user account to another without losing data.

# Creating a new account

▶

**1** Click Create New Account from the main user accounts window.

**2** When you're setting up an account you should add other people who are have full access to the PC as **Computer administrator**. This gives them full access to user account management, changes to the system and the ability to install programs and access the file structure.

**3** With a Limited account the users have full control over their account details but no-one else's. They can change their own Windows and desktop settings, access any files they create and any in shared folders. They may not be able to install programs, depending on administrator privileges.

**4** Create Account. When you've set up the account click here and it'll be available for access the next time you start Windows.

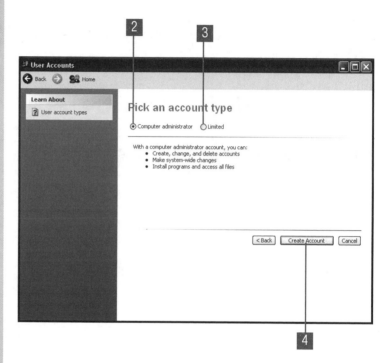

## Jargon buster

**Computer administrator** – when applied to user accounts, an administrator is a person who has full access to the entire system, including the ability to install and remove software and other administration tasks. When applied to networks and corporate systems, the administrator is the person in charge of maintaining the systems.

**Shared folder** – one that's accessible to other users of the same computer or network.

## Timesaver tip

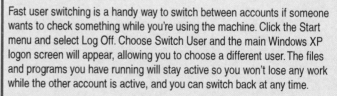

Fast user switching is a handy way to switch between accounts if someone wants to check something while you're using the machine. Click the Start menu and select Log Off. Choose Switch User and the main Windows XP logon screen will appear, allowing you to choose a different user. The files and programs you have running will stay active so you won't lose any work while the other account is active, and you can switch back at any time.

Once your user account is set up you're ready to go and can feel free to customise your Windows environment in the knowledge that your settings will be saved. If you want to change your user account image or edit your user account settings at any time this is easy to do. A handy shortcut to your user account is to open the Start menu and click the image at the top left next to the name of your user account.

# Editing user accounts

## Select an image for the account

1 Choose image. Here you can change the image that is displayed alongside your user account by choosing from any of the ones on the list that Windows supplies to help you distinguish between users.

2 Browse for more pictures. Choose this option to browse your hard drive for other images that you can use to replace your user account picture. You don't need to worry about the format or size of the image as Windows will resize it to fit best with the user account picture.

3 Change computer theme. Changing the theme of your desktop and Windows environment is one of the most instant ways of customising your account. Click this link as a shortcut to the display properties so you can do this now.

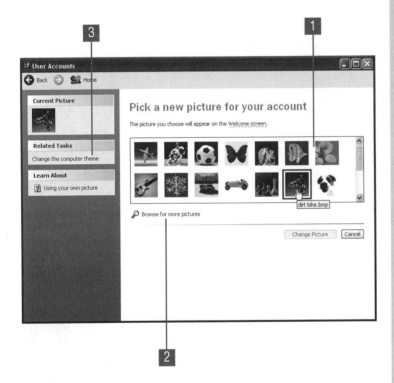

# Changing the account settings ▶

1. **Change my name.** Use this option to change the name displayed alongside your user account image.

2. **Create a password.** You can password protect your user account so other people can't use it unless they know your password. Click this option to set a password or change one you have already set up.

3. **Change my picture.** As we've shown you already, you can change the image associated with your user account from this link.

4. **Change my account type.** If you are logged on as an administrator you can change the account type here to enforce limited access.

5. If you've signed up for an **MSN passport** to use Hotmail or MSN Messenger, you can change the default passport associated with the user account here.

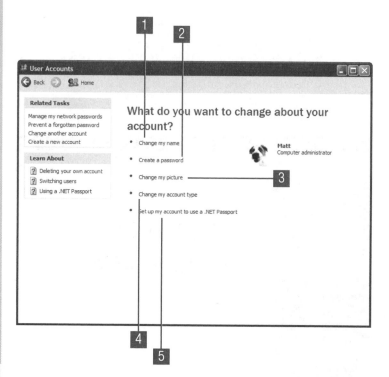

## Jargon buster

**MSN passport** – Microsoft's intended 'universal password' system, the idea being that you had one login and password that gave you access to instant messaging, email and websites. It didn't catch on quite as well as they'd hoped, and has now mostly been discontinued, though Passport accounts still work to access Hotmail, MSN Messenger and other Microsoft services.

## Important

Passwords are important wherever you use them, be it for user accounts or online banking. Try to pick a password that other people will not be able to guess, or not be able to find out easily. It's a good idea to memorise a series of passwords that you can rotate as and when you need to gain password access, using the same one for every password is dangerous. Also try to mix numbers in with letters, consider changing the letter 'o' to the number zero or the letter 'I' to the number one for example.

When your user accounts are set up and configured correctly, you can decide how Windows lets you use them by changing your logon settings. The settings you choose depend on whether you see convenience more important than security, which for the average home user is probably the case. There are two options you can choose from that change the way Windows starts up and how you control your login process. Follow the process we showed you in setting up an account to load the User Accounts window from the Control Panel and choose the Change the way users log on and off option.


# Changing logon and logoff settings

**1** Use the Welcome screen. If this setting is ticked a welcome screen will appear allowing you to simply click the name of the user account you want to log in to and enter a password if relevant. With the feature turned off you are also required to enter the name of your user account, adding to the security of the user account system.

**2** Use fast user switching. If you have chosen to enable the Welcome screen you can also enable fast user switching. With this enabled you'll be able to switch between users on the fly, without losing any settings or closing any applications or active documents.

3

# Swapping accounts with Fast User Switching

**1** Click the Start menu and choose Log Off, then select Switch User. This option will close the currently active user account and allow you to revert to another account.

**2** Choose one of the other active user accounts to switch to and you'll see the Windows environment change to reflect any differences in the desktop or theme used on this alternative account, as well as any opened applications or documents that were in this state when the account was switched from earlier. You can switch back to the other account by following the same process and choosing the other account.

## See also

Each user can customise their own desktop to suit the way they work. See Chapter 2.

Viruses are always a concern for home users, and over the last 5 years or so we've been plagued by even more infectious strains that find new and more inventive ways of making it onto our home PCs. Recent improvements to security and antivirus software has led to a quiet 6 months or so, and with Microsoft finally getting their act together and improving security through updates to their operating system, it's been less of a concern than usual. This isn't to say the average home user can relax though, the viruses are still out there and unless you're equipped with a powerful up-to-date package you could still fall foul to infection. The advent of broadband has both helped and hindered the situation. With more and more people using the internet every day, it obviously increases the likelihood of potential infection. Nearly all modern virus applications now include live update features however, and since broadband makes it so fast to download the latest updates to upgrade your software, these strains are finding it harder to make an impact. Installing and keeping a good virus-checker up-to-date is an essential but fairly straightforward process, and something every PC user should be doing. There are a number of virus-checkers around, varying from those that are free to use to 30-day trials and retail-only versions that you have to pay subscriptions for. We're going to use the virus-checker from AVG since it's free to use and offers free updates to their online virus database. Over the next few pages we'll show you how to download and update the AVG antivirus software to keep your PC safe from harm.

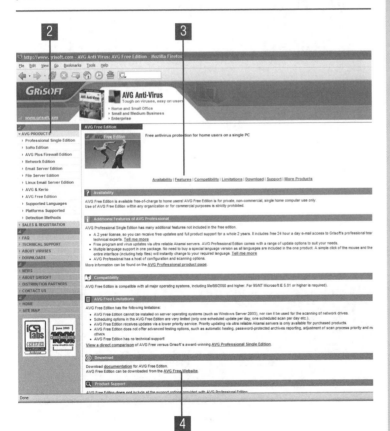

## Protecting your system from viruses

1. Browse to the Grisoft website at www.grisoft.com. Click the AVG Products link on the left and click the AVG Free Edition link near the bottom of the list.

2. Here you'll see a list of the Grisoft products. If you enjoy using the free edition you can check back here for more of their range or upgrade to the more powerful full version of their antivirus software.

3. To find out more information about the free edition of the software and how it protects your PC, click the links shown here to be taken to the appropriate area of the site.

4. When you're ready to download, click the link to be taken to the free site where you can complete your download. Click Get AVG Free and scroll to the bottom of the page to find your download link.

### Jargon buster

**Live updates** – allow a program to download new versions of itself or, in the case of spyware and antivirus tools, new information about threats to keep your system protected. Generally, live updates should be done in the background without requiring any user intervention.

# Protecting your system from viruses (cont.)

## Choose an installation type

**1** Once the software has finished downloading, double-click the icon in the download location.

**2** A wizard guides you through the install process. You can choose to install the standard version of the software, which is recommended for new users and includes the most commonly used settings.

**3** If you know what you're doing, and want further control over configuring which parts of the software are installed, you can choose the Custom Installation, which offers you option boxes to select or deselect certain elements of the software.

**4** The wizard includes Back and Next buttons to move back and forth through the installation process. Click Next to proceed after each step.

**5** At any stage click Back to move back and review your selections.

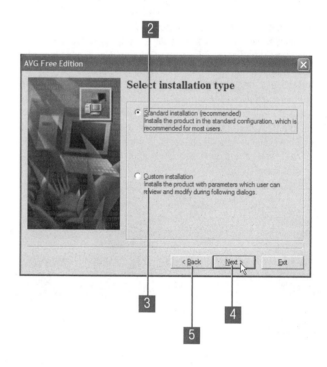

## Important

Antivirus websites like the Grisoft site update their news regularly to report new strains of viruses and any current virus alerts that their users should be aware of. It's worth checking back every now and again to find out if any recent viruses have appeared that you need to be aware of so you can update your software.

## Complete the installation

**1** Once the software is installed the software will be run and you'll see the main interface appear. This is where you control the virus software from and run scans and updates to your system.

**2** The startup wizard appears the first time you run the software and allows you to perform a Liveupdate immediately to update the software with the latest virus definitions. You should do this straight away to make sure your system is protected against the latest security risks.

**3** Again, the Back/Next wizard layout guides you through the initial setup procedure and gets the software ready to run on your system.

3

### Important

Run Live updates at regular intervals to keep your system as well protected as possible. Really these should be run every time Windows starts but if you don't connect to the internet that often they can be run intermittently to keep things in check.

# Using AVG
# Anti-Virus

**1** From the main interface, open the Test Center.

**2** Click the Virus Vault option to see results of recent scans. You can view information on the viruses that have been detected on your system, the time and date on which they were caught, as well as which files they infected.

**3** Click Help Topics for additional help with the software.

**4** The Scheduler allows you to set virus scans for certain times and help you keep your system more secure by running checks at regular intervals.

**5** A rescue disk can be created in the event that a virus prevents your system from booting. This isn't as common these days but it's worthwhile creating a disk for emergencies.

**6** Test results shows all the results of recent scans and are useful for keeping a track of how often your computer is being attacked and exactly what the software is protecting you from.

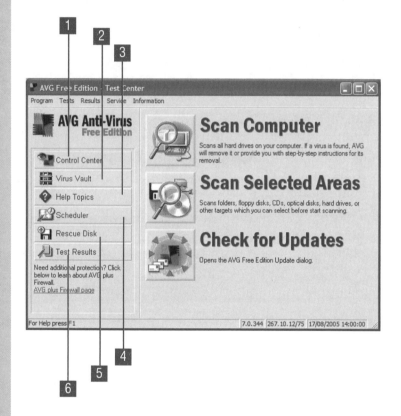

The Control Center options allow you to tailor the software for your system and decide what options you want it to use when scanning for viruses.

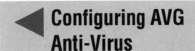

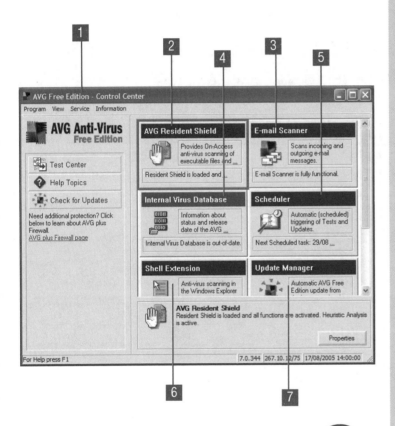

**1** Open the Control Centre.

**2** The AVG Resident Shield lets you choose which drives and files, and which areas of your system you want to scan.

**3** The Email Scanner scans incoming and outgoing mail messages. Use its options to choose which emails to scan and how to treat them if a virus is found.

**4** The Internal Virus Database stores all of the new virus definitions you can download with Live Update. It will let you know if need to run this to keep your software up to date.

**5** The Scheduler allows you to configure virus scans to run at certain times, or at regular intervals over the course of the week or month.

**6** The Shell Extension option integrates an AVG scanning option into the right-click menu on Windows Explorer.

**7** You can configure the Update Manager to run when Windows starts or whenever updates are required, and how the process should interrupt your work.

## For your information

It's worth skimming over the options available from the Control Center to set up your virus software initially before you start using it. Even if you don't understand all of the selections available, an initial look will give you a better idea of what features are available in the software and where you can go to change how AVG behaves.

# Scheduling a virus scan ▶

1. The scheduler helps you set up automated virus scanning by choosing a time or date, or regular interval on which to run the software and check your system. Schedules that you've configured appear in this list as a quick reference, along with the type and starting date of the next scan.

2. To create a new schedule, click this button and fill in the details as prompted. A scan will now run at the next configured interval.

3. To edit a current schedule, select one from the main list and click the Edit Schedule button. Depending on the type of test, you'll have different options available to change the date, time or interval of the scan, update or test.

4. To remove schedules select one from the list and click the delete button. Any scans you've set up on this schedule will no longer be run. If you have no scheduled scans in the list, you'll have to run all scans manually.

## Timesaver tip

Modern PCs are powerful enough to run virus scans with very little speed overheads on your system. If you have broadband and regularly use the internet, Liveupdates can also be performed very quickly and relatively hassle free. For this reason it's advisable to set scans and updates to run whenever you start Windows, and is the safest bet in the long run.

A rescue disk provides help in a computer emergency by booting up your system with a variety of diagnostic tools. Many programs offer the ability to create rescue disks, some of which allow you to scan for and clean viruses or restore your computer to a previous state.

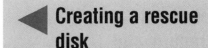

# Creating a rescue disk

1 You can choose to create a rescue disk in the event that your system is unable to boot after an infection. Click the Rescue Disk button on the main interface to bring up the Rescue Disk wizard.

2 You can choose what files you can to include on the disk, as well as an optional backup of your system files. It's advisable to leave these options checked to give you the best possible chance of recovering your system in the unlikely event of a malicious attack.

3 Use the Back and Next buttons to move back and forth through the Rescue Disk creation process.

# Viewing scan reports and changing test configuration

**1** The Test Results button will allow you to review the results of all scans on your system, including which files where infections were found. You can also change the testing configuration from here.

**2** A list of tests that have already been run appear here, at which point you can select an item from the list and use the control buttons at the bottom of the window to view more information.

**3** The Details button brings up all the test details from the scan, including when it was performed and a summary of results and objects searched.

**4** Change the test configuration here and choose which drives, and which parts of each individual drives are tested when a scan is run.

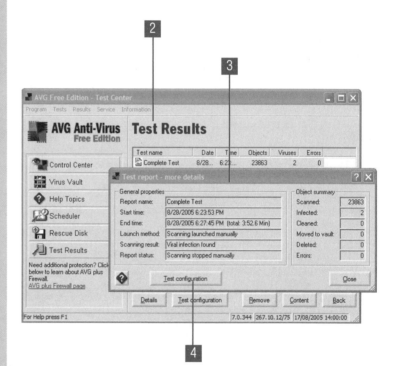

Now that your virus software is set up and ready to run, it's time to perform your first scan. This is a very straightforward task, and can be simply a case of clicking a button and waiting for the scan to complete. You can configure the software to scan certain drives or certain areas of your computer only, so it's worth taking a quick look at the options you have here to give you a better idea of how the software works.

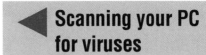

## Scanning your PC for viruses

1 Click the Scan Computer button on the main interface to run the scan. As files are being scanned they appear here along with the results for each file. This screenshot shows a finished scan.

2 A scan may take some time, so you can use the Pause or Stop buttons to halt it for whatever reason. When you run the Scan Computer tool again, you'll be asked if you want to resume from an interrupted session.

3 When the scan is finished you will have the option to display the test results if you want more information.

4 A summary of the results of the scan can be found here as well, which will hopefully read 'No Virus Found'. From this point you can either run the scan again if you're not sure a resumed scan found new files you may have installed, or close the dialog box and return to the main menu.

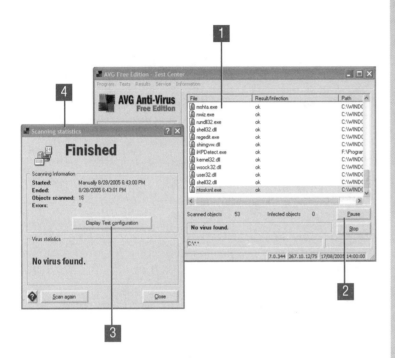

### Important

If a virus is found, you'll be offered the option to delete, fix, ignore or move it into quarantine (these are standard options that remain roughly the same across most AV applications). False hits do happen, but don't choose to ignore unless you're sure you know what the file is. Delete will obviously remove the file straight away while moving it into quarantine will stop it affecting your system but allow you to retrieve later if necessary. Fixing virus-infected files does not usually work but there's no harm in trying if the file is important.

### Jargon buster

**Quarantine** – when referring to anti-virus and spyware applications, quarantine is where all the nasty programs get dumped. A protected area of the hard disk, security tools hold infected files in quarantine so that you can examine them later or restore them if necessary without them causing damage to your system.

# Running a manual scan

We're going to run another scan now, but instead of just clicking Scan Computer we're going to configure exactly where we want the software to look for viruses.

**1** Choose Scan Selected Areas from the main interface.

**2** Under the My Computer icon you'll see your hard drives, the most common place for a virus to infect your PC. You can choose which drives to scan by clicking the corresponding box.

**3** If you're on a network you can scan the network drives or folders you have access to from your PC by clicking the '+' symbol to expand the My Network Places folder and ticking the relevant boxes.

**4** Special Locations are areas on your hard drive that are most relevant to you, and are often places that you're most likely to find viruses in. If you have multiple users on XP, you can scan the Shared Folders area in case infected files have been saved there unawares by other users of your computer.

**5** The system areas of your hard drive are where the data essential for the day-to-day running of your PC is kept. Any problems here are likely to increase substantially if they lead to malicious infection. This box should always be ticked.

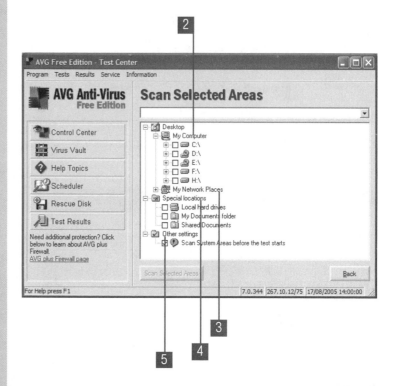

## Jargon buster

**Network Places** – a central location in Windows that shows your networked drives and computers.

## Timesaver tip

If you have a lot of data on your hard drive, or perhaps multiple hard drives attached to your system, you may find it takes a long time to scan everything for viruses. If you want to perform a faster scan for piece of mind, just choose the local hard drive – usually the C:\ drive, on which Windows is installed. This is far more likely to accumulate infections since the majority of files you'll be handling will be to and from this drive. Since Windows is run from this drive viruses that attack your operating system will also be nestling here if you're unlucky enough to attract any.

Installing antivirus software on your computer will help you stay virus-free but isn't enough protection against other internet threats. Now that broadband is the norm for new internet users, it's more important then ever to install a good firewall to help prevent attacks on your computer. A firewall acts as a buffer between your computer and the rest of the world, and can analyse and filter content by comparing the inputs and outputs on your computer with a list of 'safe' websites and computers. You can use a firewall in many ways, but most are completely configurable so you have full control over exactly who accesses your computer. Without a firewall, your PC will no doubt be subjected to attacks or intrusions, most of which will be relatively harmless, but it's not worth taking the chance and waiting for one to really do some damage. Here, we'll show you how to enable and use the Windows firewall, and how to download ZoneAlarm, the most popular free firewall around.

# Downloading and installing ZoneAlarm

## Download ZoneAlarm

1 Browse to www.ZoneAlarm.com and you'll see a range of security solutions on offer. Have a look around to see what else is on offer and download the free ZoneAlarm firewall by clicking the Download & Buy link on the left.

2 When the next page opens you'll see a range of options available. The link you're looking for is along the tabbed list at the top of the screen and reads ZoneAlarm. Click this now and you'll be taken to the free firewall page. Click the Download Now link and save the file to your computer. Once the download is completed, double-click the file to install the firewall to your computer.

# Downloading and installing ZoneAlarm (cont.)

## Install ZoneAlarm

**1** Installing the ZoneAlarm firewall is simple and you're not asked any difficult questions about setting up your computer. Simply follow through the installation wizard and fill in the details and selections as prompted on screen. When the installation is finished, ZoneAlarm will run for the first time and begin protecting your computer.

### Important

When you've finished installing ZoneAlarm it will configure itself to start every time Windows boots. You'll see the ZoneAlarm icon on the system tray, and can access the firewall to adjust settings by double-clicking this icon. You should leave ZoneAlarm running in this way while you're using Windows, since shutting it down would mean your computer is no longer protected.

ZoneAlarm uses its default security settings to protect your computer, but at some point you may need to configure or change settings on your firewall to enable programs to work correctly. It's fairly easy to do this, and is something that's well worthwhile knowing. As the number of attacks or intrusions on your computer can be quite high for many users, it's possible you may allow or block the wrong site or user and need to correct your error. You may want to increase your level of security, and should be careful to keep the software up-to-date with the Liveupdate service and keep yourself protected. Over the next few pages we'll show you how to configure your firewall to work just how you want it to with the minimum of fuss.

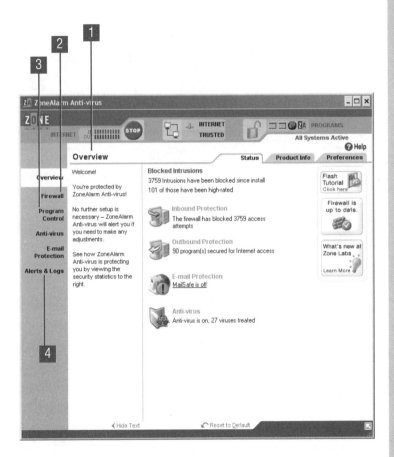

## Configuring ZoneAlarm

1. The Overview tab shows you the current status of your firewall and a summary of the configured settings. This is the main interface to the software and provides you with all you need to know at a glance. You can see the number of intrusions that have been blocked since you installed the software, how up-to-date your security is, and which programs are currently accessing the internet.

2. Click the Firewall tab and you'll be able to change the level of security your firewall is currently set at using handy slider controls. These give you an instant indication of how high your security is set with simple in-English explanations.

3. The Program Control area is where some of the more advanced settings can be altered. We'll go into this later as it's the area you're most likely to need to know. Slider controls are again available to change your level of security.

4. Alerts and Logs allow you to configure how ZoneAlarm logs the incoming and outgoing activity on your computer. You can also choose to decide how events are flagged up so you can configure how silently you want ZoneAlarm to run.

3

# Using the Overview options ▶

**1** Incoming/Outgoing activity bars are reflected on the ZoneAlarm system tray icon and give you a rough view of the activity in and out from your PC.

**2** The STOP button is an emergency switch that immediately stops any internet activity into and out of your PC. If you hit this switch any activity is frozen – handy if you feel your PC is being attacked or if you want to stop free internet activity while you're away from your machine.

**3** The Internet Lock feature is similar to the STOP button but doesn't affect all of the incoming and outgoing data on your computer. You can set specific software up with a Passlock facility to allow these applications to continue using the internet when the lock is engaged. We'll show you how later.

**4** The programs currently accessing the internet are flashed up as icons, to give you an indication of the software currently using your connection.

**5** Blocked intrusions and a summary of those programs that have outbound protection is shown in the main interface as a quick guide to how your software is performing.

**6** The web access buttons allow you to access an online tutorial to guide you through using more of ZoneAlarm's features, as well as a Liveupdate button that also informs you if your software is up-to-date. You can log onto the ZoneAlarm site from here to read more about updates and additions to their service.

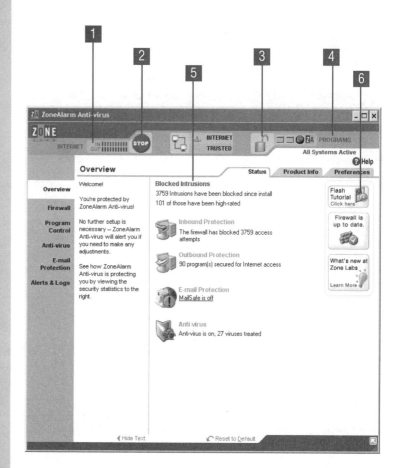

## Configuring security levels

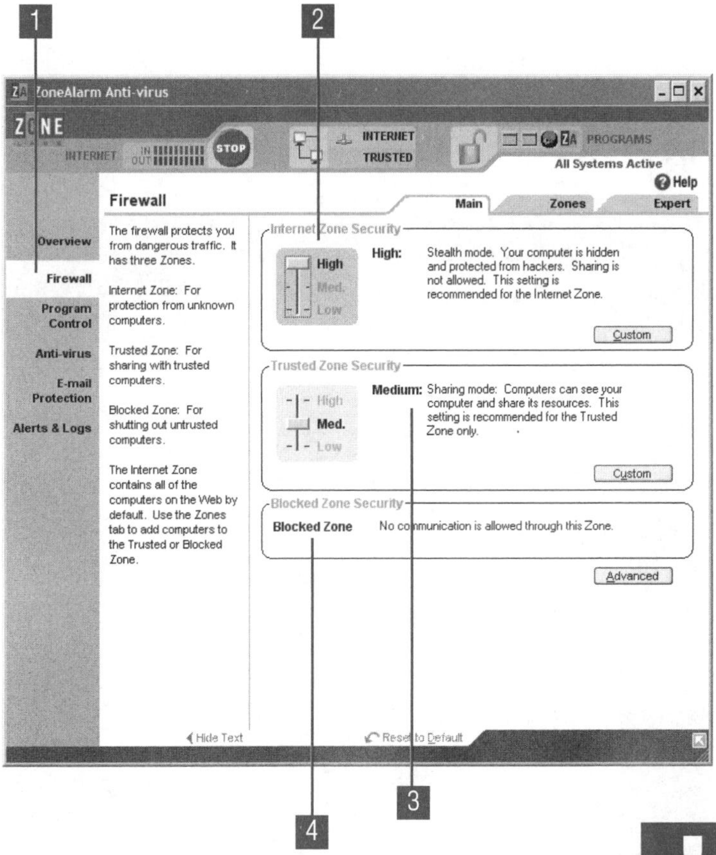

The screenshot shows:

**ZoneAlarm Anti-virus**

ZONE
INTERNET IN/OUT [STOP] INTERNET TRUSTED [icons] PROGRAMS
All Systems Active
Help

**Firewall** — Main | Zones | Expert

Overview

Firewall

Program Control

Anti-virus

E-mail Protection

Alerts & Logs

The firewall protects you from dangerous traffic. It has three Zones.

Internet Zone: For protection from unknown computers.

Trusted Zone: For sharing with trusted computers.

Blocked Zone: For shutting out untrusted computers.

The Internet Zone contains all of the computers on the Web by default. Use the Zones tab to add computers to the Trusted or Blocked Zone.

**Internet Zone Security**

High | Med. | Low

**High:** Stealth mode. Your computer is hidden and protected from hackers. Sharing is not allowed. This setting is recommended for the Internet Zone.

Custom

**Trusted Zone Security**

High | Med. | Low

**Medium:** Sharing mode: Computers can see your computer and share its resources. This setting is recommended for the Trusted Zone only.

Custom

**Blocked Zone Security**

**Blocked Zone** No communication is allowed through this Zone.

Advanced

◀ Hide Text   ↻ Reset to Default

**1** The Firewall tab allows you to change the security settings on your firewall using simple slider controls.

**2** Internet Zone security can be adjusted here. By default it is set to high, which hides your computer and connection from hackers. Since those that are placed in this zone are effectively unknown quantities, this is a wise setting to use.

**3** The Trusted Zone includes software you've specified is safe, but since some harm could potentially exist a level of security is still applied. A medium level of security is usually suitable for this setting unless you're particularly paranoid of being the attention of hackers.

**4** The Blocked Zone security is simply there as a reminder that the blocked zone exists and that there's a zero tolerance policy on access through this zone.

## ! Important

ZoneAlarm uses 'Zones' to help categorise websites into safe, potentially dangerous and dangerous. These are labelled as Trusted Zone, Internet Zone and Blocked Zone respectively. The Internet Zone is the unknown, and all computers and networks start in this zone until you move them to one of the others. The Trusted Zone are all computers and networks you specifically trust and want to share resources with. The Blocked Zone contains computers and networks that you have specified you don't trust.

# Controlling program access

It's common for new users to feel a little insecure about hackers and the like accessing their computer without permission, so it can be tempting to jack up the security to the maximum to alleviate your concerns. This isn't usually advised however, as firewalls with particularly high security can cause problems with program access and you may find applications appear to stop responding. You'll also find yourself constantly bugged for program permissions, which will be very frustrating to have to keep setting. The defaults set by ZoneAlarm should be sufficient for nearly everyone, and unless you have a particular need to change them you should leave them set as they are unless you encounter problems.

**1** The Program Control tab allows you to be more specific about exactly who and what is allowed access to your computer. Click this tab and you'll be taken to the Program Control page where you can individually configure each application.

**2** Adjusting the Program Control slider changes how frequently you're asked for confirmation of access rights for an application. If you want to be notified of every type of access, no matter how frivolous, you can set the option to high. Setting it to low will turn off both program control and the firewall and is not recommended.

**3** ZoneAlarm maintains a database of applications that are safe to use and this database can be queried to find the policy on software attempting to access the internet and automatically configure privileges for you.

**4** The automatic internet lock shuts down access for all applications except those you've specifically given a pass to. We'll show you how to give special privileges to software so they can bypass this lock a bit later.

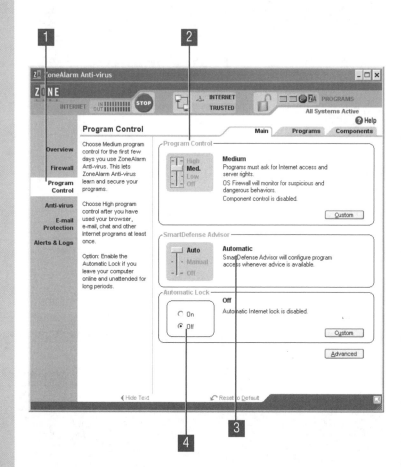

The Trust level gauge is used to determine how safe a program is to use. ZoneAlarm designates levels to software it depending on the policy stored in its database. If ZoneAlarm can't find the software it will store a question mark and you'll have to set permissions yourself when asked.

Super Access, represented by three bars, allows programs to perform suspicious and dangerous actions without seeking permission and without alerts being displayed. Trusted Acccess programs can perform suspicious but not dangerous actions without permission, Restricted Access programs are only allowed trusted-level actions, and No Access kills all access rights.

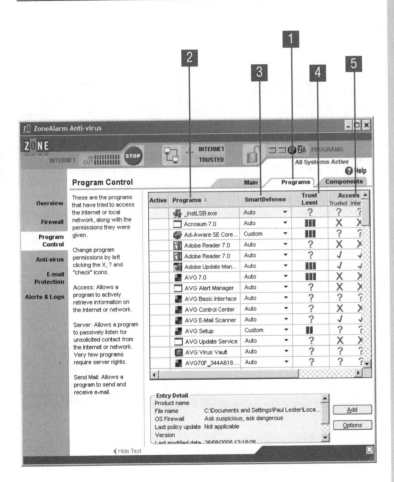

**1** In Program Control, click the Programs tab.

**2** You'll see a list of programs that have requested access to the internet from your PC. You can sort the list by program title or access settings, by clicking the column header above the appropriate list. If an application is having trouble accessing the internet, or if you've granted it permission and want to revoke it, you should be able to find it in this list.

**3** The Smart Defense option allows you to choose whether ZoneAlarm uses the rules in its safe list to configure access to this software. It can be set to Automatic or Custom, if you change any of the other settings for this software it will revert to Custom.

**4** The Trust Level of the software determines exactly what sort of activities it is allowed to perform without being flagged for permission rights. Left-click this column to see the options available, ranging from Super Access to No Access.

**5** The Access List determines what access is permitted when the software is either in the Internet or Trusted zones. Again, left click to change the current selection. If a piece of software can't access the internet or appears to freeze, it could be because they don't have access. Change access permissions to a tick here if you're sure the software is fine to access the internet.

3

# Setting individual program options

1. Right-click an application from the Programs list and click Options and you can access the option settings for this software.

2. Use the option settings to configure how the software can access the internet and other applications on your computer. Again, if applications are reporting errors or you want to grant special privileges manually you can do this here.

3. Programs can be granted a 'Passlock' here. If the Internet Lock is enabled, only software with this Passlock will be able to transmit and receive data through the firewall.

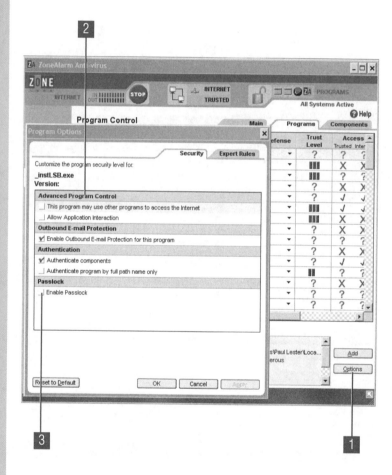

## Setting-up alerts and logs

1. Click the Alerts & Logs tab on the vertical tab list from the main interface and you'll be able to configure how alerts are generated, view logs and get more information on attacks on your computer.

2. Informational alerts appear during internet access to let you know if programs are accessing your machine, if attempts to hack your machine have been blocked and other information about connection activity. These alerts don't require an action to be taken, they are simply there to inform you, so many users like to have these turned off so as to provide an uninterrupted internet session.

3. Event Logging simply determines whether these attempts are stored in a log. If you do have notification turned off it's useful to keep Event Logging on so there is some record of attempted intrusions and activity on your computer.

4. When programs attempt to access your computer without permission an alert is generated so you can say whether or not they should be let in. You can choose to log these alerts and how many of them to save with this slider.

**1**

**2**

Z ZoneAlarm Anti-virus

ZONE

INTERNET    IN
             OUT

STOP

INTERNET
TRUSTED

PROGRAMS

All Systems Active

Help

### Alerts & Logs

Main    Log Viewer

Overview

Firewall

Program
Control

Anti-virus

E-mail
Protection

**Alerts & Logs**

Alert Events Shown: Choose which non-program alerts will generate pop-up messages.

Event Logging: Choose which non-program alerts will be recorded in the log file.

Program Logging: Choose which program alerts will be recorded in the log file.

Note: Program alerts are always shown because they require an 'Allow' or 'Deny' from you.

Alert Events Shown
- C High
- C Medium
- C Off

Do not show any informational alerts. (Program alerts will still be displayed.)

Event Logging
- C On
- C Off

Event logging is enabled.

Program Logging
- C High
- C Medium
- C Off

Log all program alerts.

Default    Custom

Advanced

Hide Text    Reset to Default

**4**

**3**

**3**

# Using the Log Viewer

**1** Choose the Log Viewer tab from the alerts and logs section.

**2** The Show Last value tells the software how many of the recent stored activities should be shown in the list.

**3** Here you can change the category the triggered alert was placed in by choosing from the list in the dropdown box.

**4** The main display here shows you all of the logged events and intrusions, including the severity rating, the type of alert and other information such as the source and destination of the event if you want to try and trace it.

**5** Choose the More Info button at the bottom and the ZoneAlarm web page will open to try and retrieve more information on the attack or event.

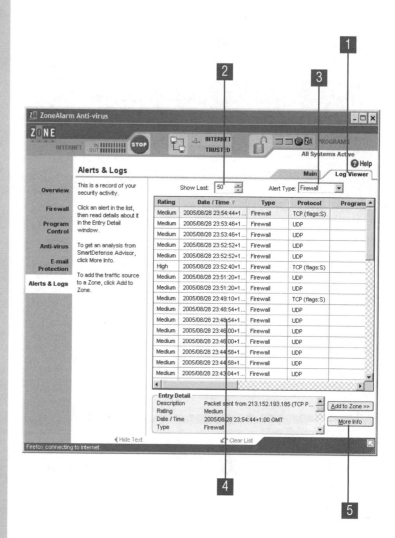

Now that you know how to set up and configure your firewall and are hopefully happy with the settings you've employed for ZoneAlarm, it's time to see it in action. You'll find yourself coming back to many of the things you've just learnt as and when alerts are raised and you see how ZoneAlarm protects your machine. You can close ZoneAlarm and leave it running in the system tray by clicking the 'X' at the top right of the interface, at which point you'll only be notified when an alert is generated. ZoneAlarm's alerts are particularly helpful as they not only describe the problem in an understandable way but give you the option to find out more from the ZoneAlarm site.

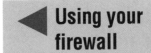

# Using your firewall

## Handle security alerts

1 A security alert is generated from the system tray ZoneAlarm icon – you'll know it as soon as one appears. You'll be informed of exactly how dangerous the behaviour might be and told what application and what part of your PC it is trying to access. Alerts flagged as 'Dangerous Behaviour' aren't cause for genuine concern half as often as their name might suggest.

2 The file being affected by the alert can be viewed by clicking the View Properties link next to the file name, if it is available.

3 To generate more information about the alert you can ask the SmartDefense Advisor, a log of applications and their security policies kept on the ZoneAlarm site.

4 The 'Apply this setting to all alerts of this nature' tickbox at the bottom of the windows is important. If you're sure this application is fine to access the internet, now and for the foreseeable future, tick this box before you click Accept or you'll be asked repeatedly every time after the software tries to access the internet again. If you're sure you'll never want the software performing the procedure outlined, tick the box before you click Deny. If you're not sure, you can just click Accept or Deny to allow or disallow the connection this time.

5 The Allow/Deny buttons control whether or not you allow the event that triggered the alert to take place.

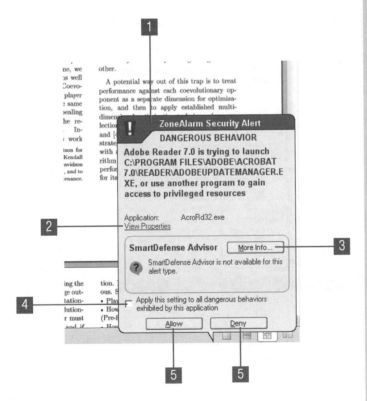

3

# Using your firewall (cont.)

It can be quite daunting for new users to make decisions on whether these various applications can or can't access the internet. ZoneAlarm does a lot of the work for you, but if after reading the alert and seeing what additional information ZoneAlarm can give you you're still not sure, there's a decision to be made. Until ZoneAlarm gets to know your PC, you'll probably see quite a lot of these alerts, and the best way to decide whether or not to permit them is to identify the software. Usually the title of the software or the information in the alert makes it obvious, otherwise check the folder of the file in question to see if that reveals what application is accessing the internet. If you know the application is safe and are happy with it going online you can accept the request. If you're never heard of the application or don't know what it does, or definitely do not want it accessing the internet you can decline the request. If at a later date you need to change these permission rights you can do it fairly easily using the Program Control options we told you about earlier.

## Investigate the security alert

1. If you click the More Info button when an alert is generated you'll be taken to the ZoneAlarm site where you can find out more about what to do next.

2. The different types of alert helps ZoneAlarm categorise the problems into various categories, so they can give you a fair idea of 'What to do' next. Read through this description to give you a better idea of the problem.

3. The Why? box gives you even further information and prepares you for some of the potential repercussions of letting the process that generated the event occur.

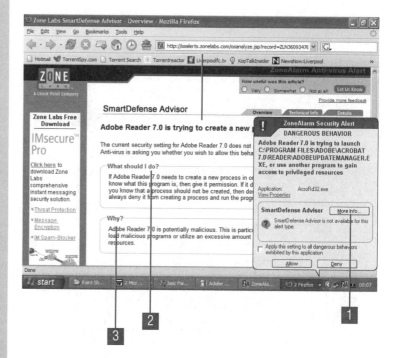

Adware and Spyware is a growing concern for internet users and as well as popping up annoying advertising and taking up bandwidth and processing time, can be used to gather information from your machine to report activities to advertising and product agencies looking to promote their services. Applications that you download and install may include adware or spyware and this is rarely flagged up in a noticeable fashion, so you may already have suspect software installed. Luckily, there are a range of programs around that will scan your machine for such problem files and give you the option to review and delete anything you don't like. With such a range of checkers and scanners available, it's often difficult to choose one to use. We've chosen Lavasoft's Ad-Aware since through tests it has been proven to recognise and remove the widest range of problem files. The software is extremely easy to use and comes with live update features to keep it up-to-date against the latest threats.

## ◀ Protecting your system from spyware

**1** First of all you'll need to download and install the Ad-Aware package. Browse to the Lavasoft website at www.lavasoft.de and you'll see they provide a wide range of security solutions, including the Ad-Aware package. Once you've downloaded the package you can install it onto your PC and perform your first scan.

**2** You'll find access to the download section towards the bottom of the main menu on the left of the site. Click the Downloads link to browse to the right page and you'll find more information on the Ad-Aware software.

**3** To download the software, you'll need to browse to the appropriate section of a download site. Click one of these links to browse straight to this page.

### Jargon buster

**Adware** – installed along with other applications and delivers adverts through the application window or pop-up windows. Often Adware is more of an annoyance than a real threat, as many free programs use it to bring in money.

**Spyware** – applications that monitor your computer and return data about your activities to the people who created them. Often combined with adware. Many spyware applications are malicious, intrusive and incredibly stubborn, proving extremely difficult to remove once they're into your PC. There is a thin line between spyware and virus.

# Downloading Ad-Aware from Download.com

When the software download has finished, double-click the icon to install the package and you'll see a typical installation wizard appear. Click the Next button to follow through the wizard and complete installation on your computer. Once the software is installed it's easy to perform a quick scan of your system. We'll take a look at the scanning options available, show you how to perform a fast scan and a more detailed scan of your system, and take a look at what options are available to customise your system scan. A bit later we'll look at customising the software further a look at the other features such as the Ad-Watch tool that can help protect your system.

1. At the www.download.com download site you can read more information about the product as well as user ratings before you download.

2. Click the Download Now link to download the software to your hard drive so that you can install it onto your system.

## ! Important

Like antivirus software and firewalls, Ad-Aware continues to run in the background to keep your machine safe. The Ad-Watch product in particular stays resident in your system tray and will alert you as and when problems occur. Ad-Aware retains no such obvious interface, but you can set up system scans on startup and 'Smartscanning', an automatically scheduled scan to take place at an opportune time when Windows is running. These smartscans run in the background and help to keep your machine ad-free on a more permanent basis. Despite this, you should load and run Ad-Aware intermittently for your own peace of mind, and run full system scans whenever the opportunity arises.

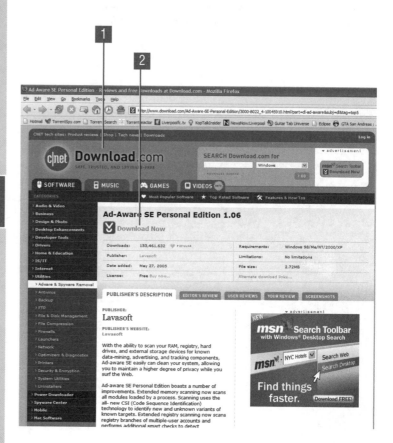

## Use Ad-Aware

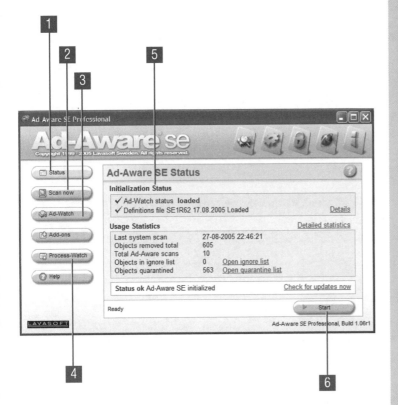

1 Click the Status button and you'll be taken to this interface, where you can view summaries of recent scans and perform a quick scan of your system straight away.

2 The Scan Now button takes you to the scan configuration screen, where you can gain more control over a scan.

3 Click Ad-Watch to launch the Ad-Watch tool, a useful add-on that can help prevent problem files from reaching your system in the first place by blocking suspicious behaviour and requesting permission from you before changes are made to your machine.

4 The Process-Watch is a built-in utility that keeps an eye on processes currently running on your machine. You can use this tool to terminate problem processes, and find out what other files they're accessing on your system.

5 Initialization Status shows whether Ad-Watch is active and gives you the date of the current spyware definition file.

6 The Start button takes you to the scan menu so you can choose how to scan your system.

# Using Ad-Aware shortcut buttons

**1** Ad-Watch. This shortcut to the Ad-Watch tool loads or restores the Ad-Watch tool for you to review activities and change settings.

**2** This button opens the Ad-Aware configuration window, and allows you to adjust settings such as logfiles, how the software handles ads, what parts of your hard drive are scanned, how the software interacts with Windows and a range of other settings to help you control the software.

**3** The Quarantine manager contains all of the ads or troublesome files that have been removed from your system and quarantined. You can check back here at any point to see exactly what adware, spyware or additional software has been found on your system through Ad-Aware's scans.

**4** Like virus software, Ad-Aware can be updated using a live update tool to make sure that it has all of the latest definitions and can catch the very latest adware and spyware. Select this option and click Connect to check the Ad-Aware website for updates.

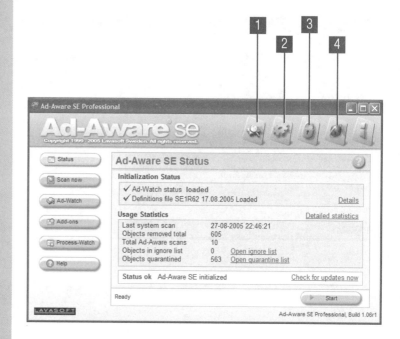

## Configuring Ad-Aware

**1** Click the Options button from the main interface.

**2** The General options allow you to control logfiles and set definition reminders to prompt you to perform LiveUpdate.

**3** Scanning options help you choose which files and which parts of your system to include in scans.

**4** Click the Advanced options to control shell integration and the detail of the logfiles created by the software.

**5** Click the Startup button to set the software to start automatically with Windows or to enable smart scanning for automatic scanning at appropriate times. You can also set an automatic Liveupdate check to search for new definitions.

**6** The Defaults button lets you change all of Ad-Aware's setting back to default in case you can't remember what you've changed.

**7** You can change the appearance of the software and its behaviour when problem files are detected through the Interface menu.

**8** The Tweak menu is for more advanced users and gives you the ability to fine-tune scans and the ways the software interacts with your system.

3

---

Lavasoft Ad-Aware SE

# Ad-Aware se
Copyright 1999 - 2005 Lavasoft Sweden. All rights reserved.

**2** General
**3** Scanning
**4** Advanced
**5** Startup
**6** Defaults
**7** Interface
**8** Tweak

## General Settings

**Safety**
- ✓ Automatically save logfile
- ✓ Automatically quarantine objects prior to removal
- ✓ Safe mode (always request confirmation)

**Definitions**
- ✓ Prompt to update outdated definitions
- Consider definitions outdated after `14` days

**Write logfiles to:**
`C:\Documents and Settings\Paul Lester\Application Data\La`

**Using definitions file:**
`C:\PROGRA~1\Lavasoft\AD-AWA~1\defs.ref`

Click "Proceed" to save settings    ✓ Proceed

LAVASOFT

# Preparing a system scan

**1** From the main menu, click the Scan Now button to move the scanning menu, where you can start system scans or customise your scans to include or skip specific files.

**2** You have four options for scanning your machine here. Smart system scans are quick scans that can double-check for errors that may not have been picked up since the last full scan. The in-depth scan scans your whole computer for spyware infections. If you believe your computer may be infected with spyware you should choose this option. The custom scanning allows you to configure which files are included in the scan, and the ADS (Alternate Data Streams) scan is a two-phase scan that can pick up files missed by the regular scans.

**3** Negligible entries and low-risk threats are not considered to be real threats to your system, but you can enable these options to include these items in any scan and remove them if desired.

**4** Click this button to run a scan once you're happy with the options you've chosen.

## Important

Smart scans are great for a quick analysis of your system, but it's important to perform full system scans on a regular basis as well. If you're performed a full scan recently you can double-check with the smart scan, but if you suspect that you are infected with adware or spyware, or you have installed a lot of new software on your system recently you should run a full scan.

**1** If you chose the custom scan you'll see the customise link alongside that allows you to change the setting for the software. Here you can choose to scan archives, exclude non-executable files, which are less likely to be problematic, or exclude files over a certain size. You can also choose specific files or folders to scan if you expect a particular area of your hard drive to be at risk.

**2** These options allow you to choose which parts of your memory or the registry are included in scans.

**3** When you're happy with your settings, click the Proceed button to perform a custom scan.

**3**

Lavasoft Ad-Aware SE

**Ad-Aware se**
Copyright 1999 - 2005 Lavasoft Sweden. All rights reserved.

General
Scanning
Advanced
Startup
Defaults
Interface
Tweak

**Scan Settings**

**Drives, Folders & Files**
- Scan within archives
- Skip non-executable files
- Skip files larger than  4096  kB
- Select drives & folders to scan

**Memory & Registry**
- Scan active processes
- Scan registry
- Deep-scan registry
- Scan my IE Favorites for banned URLs
- Scan my Hosts file

Click "Proceed" to save settings     ✓ Proceed

LAVASOFT

# Running a system scan

1. When scanning your machine, the main Ad-Aware window will update you with the progress of your scan, and keep you informed here of the current operation and the name of the file currently being scanned.

2. Here you'll see a summary of the total number of **processes** running and the total number of **modules**. As and when problems are found they are reported here along the way.

3. You can see how many of the different types of potentially problematic files are infecting your system as these lists update.

4. Scans can take some time, particularly full system scans, so use this button to cancel the current scan. You can still Quarantine or remove the files that have been found so far, but you should run another scan at the earliest opportunity to finish the process.

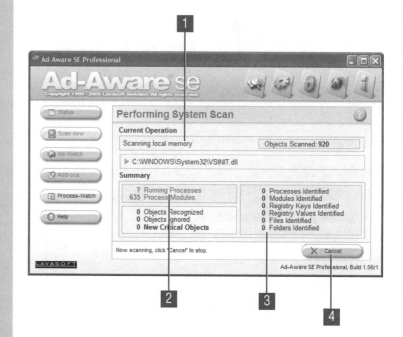

## Jargon buster

**Module** – a program may be constructed from several linked modules, which provide different functions and are themselves small applications.

**Process** – a program that's currently running. Some background programs are constantly running while you're in Windows.

If you've just performed your first scan, you're most likely to find quite a few files on your system that have been detected by the software as problematic. Luckily, removing or quarantining the files is very easy, and there's even a quarantine manager so that you can review any files that have been detected and changed by the software. We'll show you how to handle the results of your first scan and where to go from there.

# Examining your scan results

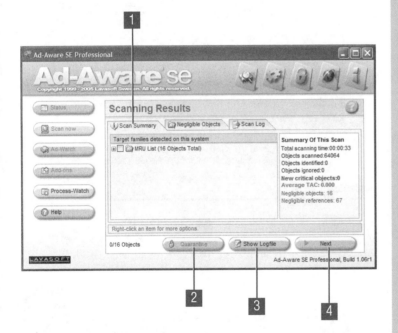

**1** When a scan is completed you'll be taken to a results screen that looks something like this. The Scan Summary shows you all of the potentially dangerous files, or if the option was selected, negligible risk files found on your system. Tick the boxes alongside the files you want to treat.

**2** If you don't want to delete the files, you can place them in Quarantine, which will isolate and backup the items you've selected so you can reinstall them at a later time if you want to. Items in the Quarantine folder are encrypted and compressed to save space, and can only be restored by Ad-Aware. Anything in Quarantine poses no threat to your computer.

**3** To find out more information on the results of your scan click the Show Logfile button to open the scan log.

**4** To remove the files from your computer completely, make sure they are ticked in the scan results window and click the Next button. You'll then be asked if you want to remove the files and your scan and clean is complete.

# Using the Quarantine Manager

1. To open the Quarantine Manager, click the icon showing the padlock from the row at the top of the main interface.

2. The Quarantine Manager lets you view and restore or remove any items that have been placed into Quarantine as the result of a scan. You can see the items in the list in this main window, select one to activate it and enable your options.

3. The Item Log provides you with all the information gathered on the item by the scan and exactly why the item was deemed as a problem file.

4. Click the Delete button to remove the file from your system for good. Do this if you're sure you won't want to restore it in future and that its removal won't affect the stable operation of your system.

5. If you've found that certain programs won't run since this item has been quarantined, you can restore it by clicking the Restore button.

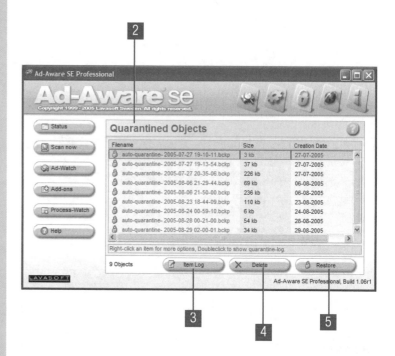

## Important

Some software requires specific adware or spyware to be installed on your system for it to run properly, and will check for this software whenever you try and execute the program. For this reason, if you remove the adware or spyware the application may not run. There is rarely a way around this, as the software is specifically configured to run alongside the problem files. If you've removed the files, you may need to reinstall the application that needs them from scratch in order to run it successfully again. If you're quarantined the items you can restore them to regain access to that particular application.

Additional tools are available with Ad-Aware that can further enhance the security of your system and provide you with more information on the files and processes running. Ad-Watch acts as a barrier between your computer and files that try to adjust system settings or gather information from your PC. While Ad-Aware can clean and remove files once they have arrived on your computer, Ad-Watch can prevent them from even getting there in the first place. Ad-Watch can load with Windows and run in the background, informing you to choose whether to let suspect files affect your system. The Process-Watch is a powerful process viewer/manager that allows browsing, scanning and termination of processes on your system, and provides you with more information on their associated modules.

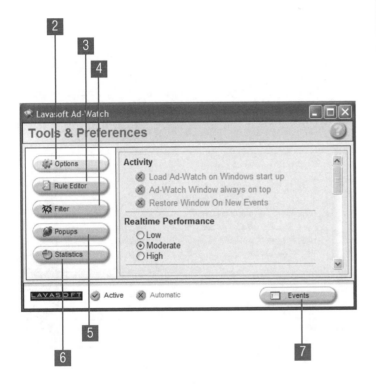

### Jargon buster

**Filter** – a specific pattern or attribute that sorts data based on the parameters given. Think of it like digitally sifting flour, it removes the lumps and only gives you exactly what you want!

# Protecting your system with Ad-Watch

## Configure Ad-Watch

**1** Ad-Watch options can be accessed by clicking the Tools button at the bottom right. If the button reads Events, you are already at the options window.

**2** You can choose when Ad-Watch is active, what parts of your system to watch, and which log reports are filed.

**3** You can use the Rule Editor to configure Ad-Watch to automatically allow specific changes to the registry. Certain registry keys or values can be changed without the software prompting you for permission.

**4** If you choose to allow processes when permission is requested, those you allow are saved in the filter list for you to review.

**5** Popups are annoying windows that appear advertising a product or service while you're browsing the internet. Ad-Watch will block these for you. The Popups option is effectively a black list of websites that Ad-Watch blocks for you. Sites can be added or removed from the list easily so you have full control over which sites can interact with your computer.

**6** The Statistics window shows the total statistics for Ad-Watch blocking and filtering.

**7** Click the Events button to switch to the main event log window. Here Ad-Watch shows all events that have been logged during the session.

# Protecting your system with Ad-Watch (cont.)

## Respond to an Ad-Watch alarm

**1** When Ad-Watch detects that another software package is attempting to change a setting on your computer, or when an intrusion is detected that you should be notified of, a warning window appears. You should get some idea of exactly where the change would take place from the information in this message to give you an idea of whether or not to proceed.

**2** If you need further advice on what to do next, click this option to retrieve further information.

**3** You need to decide at this point whether or not to accept the change to your system. If you want to allow or decline this change every time, click the Automatic icon to turn it green. After you've made your selection the program requesting access will either be permitted or granted access on a permanent or temporary basis.

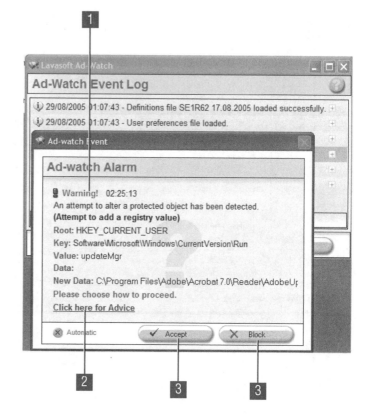

## Monitoring your system with Process-Watch

1. To load the Process-Watch tool, click the Process-Watch button on the main interface.

2. The main window on the Process-Watch interface shows you which processes are currently running along with further information about these processes for diagnostic purposes.

3. The modules display shows you which modules are currently associated with the process you have selected in the processes box above. You can unload a module if you suspect it to be causing problems by selecting it in this window, right-clicking and choosing Unload Module.

4. Click the Refresh button to create a new process snapshot and refresh all information in both the process and module window.

5. The Scan All option scans executable files for all processes, and deactivates the filtering activated by default. Any suspected processes are listed in red for you to investigate further.

6. Click the Terminate button to terminate the selected process.

### Important

Terminating processes and unloading modules if you're not sure what you are doing could lead to system instability and cause applications to crash. You should save all of your work before attempting to manipulate any files using the Process-Watch tool and only do so if you have good reason to suspect a process or module is causing problems.

# Monitoring your system with Process-Watch (cont.)

## Make changes to processes

**1** Right-click a process or module to access further functions.

**2** You'll find shortcuts to source folders and file properties so you can retrieve quick information on the processes displayed.

**3** Export or print reports of processes currently running. These reports can be invaluable diagnostic tools if you're reporting your problem online or to a third party.

**4** If you right-click a module you're presented with a similar list, but with the option of unloading the module in question, dumping the process memory and displaying it in a window, or dumping the process and saving it to disk as a file.

Protecting your PC against external threats is a great way to beef up security, and so far we've looked at how to do this with a firewall, virus scanner and what can keep adware and spyware at bay. What we haven't touched on yet is security for your PC against local threats, such as those posed by shared machines. Again, a range of software packages are around that offer you a range of security services but we're using the WinGuard software for its ease of use and ability to protect a number of different areas of your system all from one interface. We'll be showing you how to use this software to prevent access to applications and various areas of your Window operating system, and how to encrypt sensitive files with your own personal passwords.

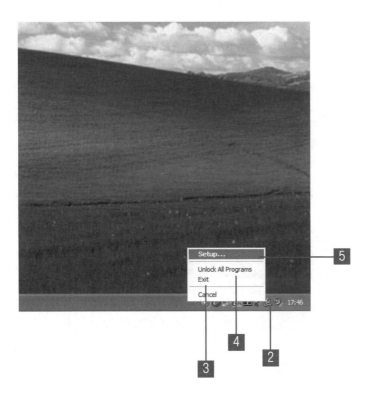

# Protecting your system with passwords and encryption

## Get started with WinGuard

**1** Download and install the WinGuard software from www.download.com. WinGuard integrates with your system in a number of ways, and when run initially you won't actually see an interface appear. Instead, a system tray icon controls access to the software.

**2** The WinGuard icon on the scrollbar looks like a small key and padlock. Right-click this icon to bring up the WinGuard menu.

**3** To exit the software and unload any protection to files or applications you may have added, click the Exit button here.

**4** The Unlock All Programs option removes any protection you've added to Windows applications so anyone can access them.

**5** Click the Setup button to open the main interface for the software and get started with protecting your files and applications.

**6** Whenever the software loads or you try to adjust any settings or see the main menu you'll be asked for a password. When you first use the software the default password is printed on screen so you know how to get into the software the first time around. Type in the password now and click OK to open the setup menu.

# Password protecting your applications

We've shown you how to set up individual user accounts on Windows XP to help restrict access to your files and folders, but there's no harm in adding extra security to keep sensitive data private. If you have a number of files or folders that you'd like to keep away from prying eyes, you can use an encryption service to make sure only you can open these files. You can also restrict access to other applications on your computer to prevent other users from changing your machine or using services or applications without permission.

**1** When the interface appears you'll be taken to the Home tab by default. Here you can see your current protection level, and a tabbed interface that'll guide you around the software. Click Program Protection.

**2** You'll see a list of common Windows applications currently set up to use password protection. Tick those on the list that you want to restrict access to. Typically the most common ones you'd like to restrict are those that allow the user to make changes to the Windows system, like the Control Panel or command line prompt.

**3** Click the Add button to add new software to the list so you can protect new applications that you've installed on your system.

**4** Click the Remove button to remove an item from this list.

**5** Click the Ignore button to specify applications that you'd like to ignore password protection for. This ensures that these applications can be loaded without being prompted.

**6** None of the changes you've made will come into place until you click the Apply button, at which point the chosen applications will be locked for access unless you have a password.

**7** Open a program. You'll be greeted with the standard WinGuard password dialog. Type the password and your application will start.

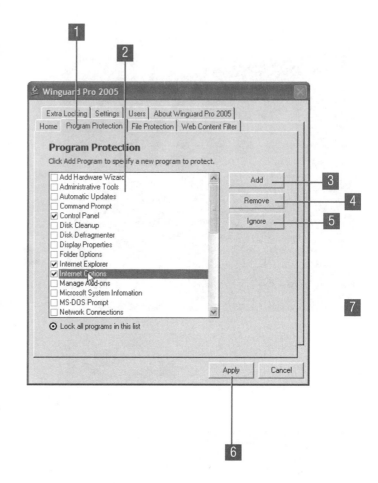

One of the ways to protect files is by encryption, the conversion of data into a scrambled code, so that it cannot be read by normal means. Encrypted data must be unscrambled before it can be accessed. Most encryption is not completely foolproof but modern encryption techniques take a large amount of skill and computing power to crack.

## Protecting files and folders

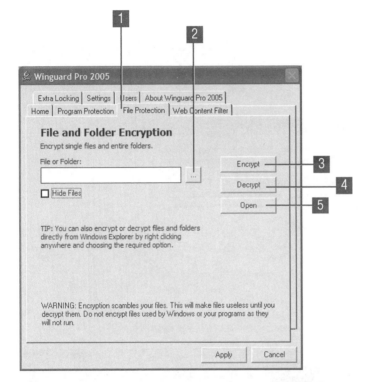

1 Choose the File Protection tab and we'll show you how to encrypt individual files or folders.

2 Click the three dots alongside the File or Folder box and browse to a folder on your hard drive that contains files you'd like to encrypt.

3 Choose the Encrypt button to encrypt the contents. After encryption you won't be able to open these files unless you decrypt them through the software.

4 Click the Decrypt button to remove encryption you've previous applied using the software so the files can be opened again.

5 Click the Open button as a shortcut to open the folder you're currently working with.

6 If you click the Open button to open the folder or browse to the folder after you've encrypted it, you'll find that each file now has the '.loc' extension. The files can't be opened by their original application, and the only way to read these files again is to use the decrypt option within the software.

**!**

## Important

Usually the only files you'll need to encrypt on a personal computer are those you've created yourself. Be careful when browsing around for files to encrypt. If you select system files, modules or essential areas of your machine Windows needs to be able to read in order to run with stability, you may have problems since your operating system is unable to read encrypted files.

## Jargon buster

**Encryption** – the conversion of data into a scrambled code, so that it cannot be read by normal means. Most encryption is not completely foolproof but modern techniques take a large amount of skill and computing power to crack.

# Blocking websites

If you have young children using the computer, you'll want to ensure they don't stumble across any unsuitable content while browsing the web. WinGuard includes a simple web content filter that lets you block sites using keywords. It's not as efficient as some specialised filtering tools but works well as a low-tech solution.

**1** The Web Content Filter allows you to filter web pages based on keywords you specify in order to prevent minors or other users access potentially inappropriate content.

**2** The main window on this tab will show a list of keywords you've decided to add to the web filter. If these words are detected on any websites that other users try to access, they'll be prompted for a password before the page will open.

**3** Click the Add button to add new keywords to the list.

**4** Click Remove to remove any existing keywords.

**5** When you choose to Add an item, an additional window appears where you can type the keywords you wish to ban.

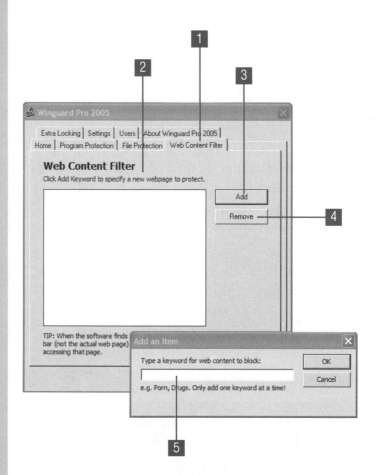

Find out how to lock additional applications and how to change the way the software behaves. You'll also need to know how to change the default password for access to the WinGuard software, and how to change the password used to access locked applications.

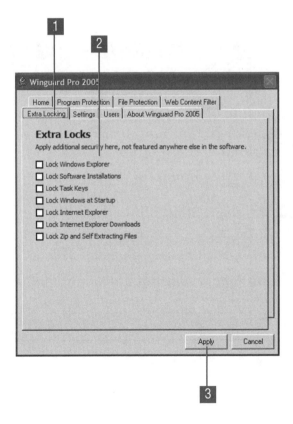

**1** Click the Extra Locking tab to view additional Windows tools and applications you can lock with the software.

**2** Tick the boxes alongside the tools you want to add password access to.

**3** Again, click the Apply button to apply the changes you've made and force the ticked applications to request a password before they open.

3

# Changing
# WinGuard settings

**1** Choose the Settings tab to access vital settings for the WinGuard software including changing the default password for setup and program access.

**2** The Password timer setting states how long the password prompt stays displayed for.

**3** If you've used the Unlock All command from the system tray icon, this timer relocks everything back to its original state after the number of minutes you specify here.

**4** This option removes the system tray icon from your desktop.

**5** The final two options prevent users from unlocking programs and creating a blank screen whenever a password is required.

**6** The Setup Tool password is the one you need when you open the software interface from the system tray icon. Users with this password can encrypt and decrypt files, change any of the settings and do everything covered here. Only administrators should know this password.

**7** The Locked Items password is the one required whenever a locked application or window tries to open. You can give the locked items password to any users you wish to have access to software and Windows settings, but do now wish to have access to the settings within the WinGuard software.

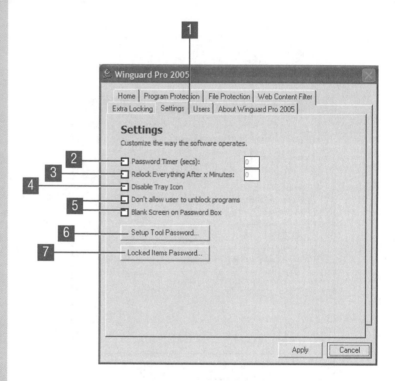

# Managing software and files

## Introduction

Anyone who was using computers back in the days of Windows 3.1 or DOS will remember the installation and uninstall routines, which generally involved copying all the files to the hard disk and then deleting them when no longer needed. Nowadays it's all automatic and we simply need to run the installation file and watch as the files are copied across, then run the uninstall procedure to remove them again. Windows even has a dedicated option for managing installed applications. In this chapter we'll take you through a sample install and uninstall procedure to demonstrate what's involved and also look at how you can manage the files on your hard disk by moving, copying and deleting them and creating new folders and shortcuts, as well as searching your computer for that hard-to-find data.

## What you'll do

**Install applications**

**Patch and update software**

**Remove applications from your PC**

**Open and modify files**

**Move and copy files**

**Delete files**

**Create new files, folders and shortcuts**

**Search your computer**

### Timesaver tip

Before heading into the details of how to install, move and copy files, we will take the time to stress the importance of an organised and consistent filing system. Although there are sophisticated search features you can use, you don't want to be resorting to them every time.

# Installing applications

Installing applications on a modern PC is, generally, a very simple process that involves clicking a few Next buttons and selecting some options. To demonstrate, we're going to step through the installation of WinZip, the popular file compression tool. Obviously it's not within the scope of this book to take you through every possible installation procedure you'll encounter, but generally speaking once you've seen one you've seen them all. Certain installations will be more complex of course, Microsoft Office, for example, includes the option of a custom installation whereby you can select which individual components are used, but even then it's relatively user-friendly.

## Run the installation file

**1** Locate the executable installation file (it will end in **.EXE** or .MSI) for the program you wish to install and double-click it to start. Programs on CD should start automatically when you place the disk in your computer.

**2** You'll usually get a dialog or two introducing the program. In this example we click Setup to continue or Cancel to end the installation.

## Jargon buster

**Freeware** – free software. Some have 'Pro' features that are unlocked by paying a registration fee.

**EXE** – a file with the .EXE extension means that it is an executable program file, a self-contained program that will run on its own. This can be a software installation package or application.

**Extension** – the letters after a filename that tell you what kind of data the file contains. For example '.jpg' is a JPEG image and '.txt' is a text file.

**Shareware** – trial software that can be used until a certain expiry date, at which point you must pay to continue using it.

**3** If it asks where you want to install the program, choose Browse to select an alternative location. The Program Files folder is the default for most recent applications. To make things simple it's best to keep all your applications in one place.

**WinZip Setup**

Setup will install WinZip into the following folder, which it will create if necessary.

If you want to install WinZip in a different folder and/or drive, type the name of the folder below:

Install to:

C:\Program Files\WinZip       Browse...

OK       Cancel

**3**

### Did you know?

Don't fancy shelling out for the pricey Microsoft Office? OpenOffice (www.openoffice.org) is a free, open-source Office suite that includes fully-featured word processor, spreadsheet, database and image editor. You can also play music and video files for free using Winamp (www.winamp.com) or edit images using the powerful and bizarrely named GIMP (www.gimp.org). All these are free alternatives to commercial applications. Just about any major program out there has a freeware clone, so if you're strapped for cash and in dire need of software this is one option. See the final chapter for more places to get great software.

### For your information

The best place to find new software is of course the internet, where there are thousands upon thousands of sites offering downloads of **freeware** and shareware. Freeware is free software that costs nothing to use. Often there will be a 'Pro' version of the tool which must be paid for but offers more features. **Shareware** is a term to trial programs. Sometimes they are unrestricted trials which must be purchased after a certain length of time; others have features that are disabled until you register.

Some of the most popular download sites are www.download.com, www.tucows.com and www.majorgeeks.com. You can download a free trial for WinZip from any of those sites or from its official homepage at www.winzip.com.

**4**

# Installing applications (cont.)

## Read the license agreement

**1** Before the installation begins you will almost always be shown a License Agreement, which lays out what you can and cannot do with the program. If you really don't agree with the terms, click No to cancel. Otherwise Yes will take you to the next step.

**2** Click the Next buttons to continue through the installation. Some apps will start to install almost immediately while others, such as WinZip, include options like these asking you to select an interface style.

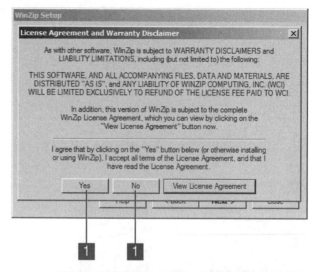

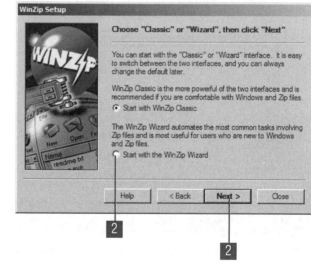

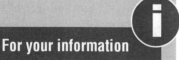

### For your information

If you click No at the License Agreement dialog box, the software will not be installed.

## Jargon buster

**License agreement** – the legalese that appears whenever you install software and lays out exactly what you can and can't do with an application. For the average home user there's probably not much of relevance or interest, if you're planning on using a program in a business capacity however you might want to have a read as some free applications require business users to purchase a license.

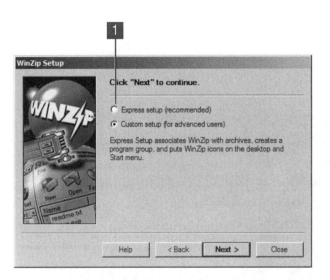

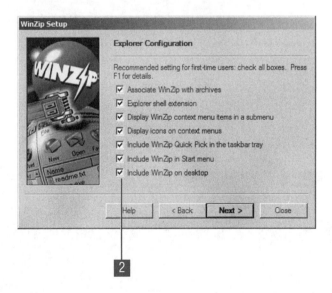

## Choose an installation type

1 You'll sometimes be asked whether you want a custom installation or express installation. Express automatically configures the program using the most common settings, while Custom gives you full control over the installation steps.

2 If you've chosen the Custom installation you'll be able to customise the behaviour of the application during installation. With WinZip, this involves selecting whether you want a desktop and quick launch icon or Explorer extension, among others.

**4**

## Timesaver tip

Although Custom installations are marked for 'Advanced Users', we'd recommend selecting this option whenever it is available. It gives you a far greater level of control over the way the program behaves, especially in regards to file associations and operating system integration. It can save you hassle later on especially when some programs don't make it entirely obvious how to reverse the choices made during installation.

**Managing software and files 113**

# Installing applications (cont.)

## Complete the installation

**1** If you chose to associate files with WinZip then you'll get the option of selecting which files are associated. For more information on file associations see the section on files later in this chapter. You can click Next to just accept the default selections for associations

**2** The final step before WinZip installs asks if you want to create a program group and icons in the Start menu.

**3** Click the Program Locations button to configure external applications for handling file types WinZip does not recognise. Many applications will ask you to do this, often for specifying a virus scanner.

**4** Once the installation process is finished your program is ready to run. You can find your application either via a shortcut in the quick launch bar, start menu or on the desktop, depending on the options you chose during installation, or you can navigate to the directory where its files are stored.

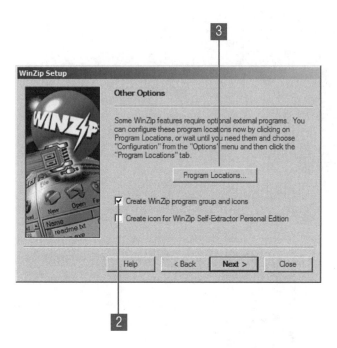

## Important

Before running any software application you should always ensure it is free of viruses and other harmful software. Virus scanners should always be configured to manually scan files as they're accessed, but you can run a manual scan anytime you like and this will often be available as an option in the context menu if you right-click on a file. Spyware is also a risk. If the spyware is legitimate the company is required to ask you to 'opt-in' and agree to them installing it. Check the license agreement and installation options for mentions of additional software, especially web browser and desktop toolbars. Others will install spyware without permission. See the previous chapter for more information on viruses and spyware.

**Patches** are a necessary evil when using a PC. It can be a pain to constantly ensure that every one of your programs is up-to-date but it's absolutely vital for ensuring the security and smooth running of your system. It's not all bad, either, as some patches aren't always used to fix holes but to give your program new features. Some require you to download a newer version of the installation file while others can be patched either automatically via a central server or by downloading a small patch file that is simply run and installed like any other program.

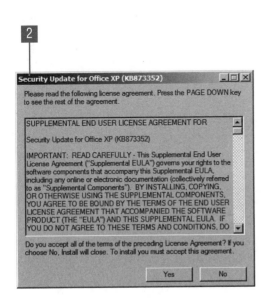

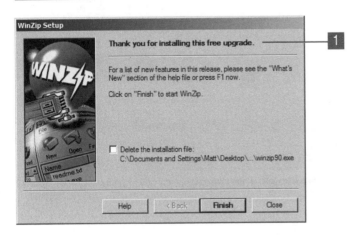

**1** Some programs, such as WinZip, can be updated by downloading the newer version and installing it over the top of the previous one. Doing this should usually retain important details like registration keys and settings. If your program is several versions old however, it may be a good idea to uninstall it before installing the update. In our example, we have updated WinZip by installing the latest version, available on the WinZip homepage.

**2** A patch will update certain parts of the application without requiring you to do a complete reinstall. They are most often used for large commercial packages where it's not possible or unrealistic to download a complete new version of the program. Here, we're applying a security patch to Microsoft Office, downloaded from Microsoft's Windows Update site.

**4**

### Jargon buster

**Patch** – software updates that fix holes or introduce new features into a program.

# Patching and updating software (cont.)

Many applications will communicate with a central server to inform you about new updates. It's a good idea to enable this option or allow the program to connect to its server since you'll be alerted to critical security updates. Just as Windows XP suffers from security problems, many programs have holes that are diskovered and fixed later on, so as well as making sure you've got the latest features software patches will help keep your system secure.

## Use live update

**1** The easiest way to update software is using live or **auto-update** functions, if they're available. These will connect to a server, download the latest updates and install them without you needing to do much at all. We've used Lavasoft's anti-spyware tool Ad-Aware, which can download new updates to its definition files without needing a reinstall.

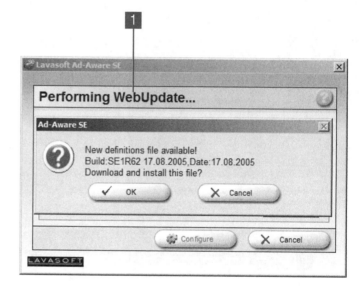

### Jargon buster

**Auto-update** – software that auto-updates will download and install the latest version of itself, often without user-intervention. Sometimes called a live update.

116

Once you no longer need an application, you should remove it from your system to save hard disk space. All applications with an install procedure will (or should) make it simple to remove them when you're done. Add/Remove Programs, in the Control Panel, is the central location for uninstalling programs. Once a program is installed it will be listed in Add/Remove Programs where it can be uninstalled or modified. Add/Remove programs also contains options for changing the default applications for web browsing, email and other tasks and making changes to Windows tools and features.

# Removing applications from your PC

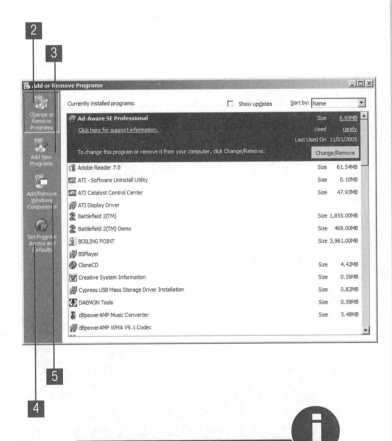

## Use Add/Remove Programs

1. Open up Control Panel, find Add/Remove Programs and double-click it.

2. In Add/Remove Programs, you have several buttons down the left side. Change or Remove Programs is the default view and lists all installed applications on your PC (provided that they have registered themselves with the system) and allows you to check their file size and make changes, like uninstalling, changing settings or sometimes reinstalling to fix problems.

3. Add New Programs opens a helper for programs on disk or from Windows Update. There is no real reason to use this instead of visiting Windows Update or running the EXE off a disk.

4. Add/Remove Windows Components lets you install and uninstall the applications and tools included with Windows. If you find something is missing because it wasn't selected during the initial Windows setup, it can be added through here.

5. Set Program Access and Defaults allows the default settings for web browsers, media player and others to be changed.

## For your information

The Set Program Access and Defaults option was introduced with Service Pack 1 following an anti-trust case bought against Microsoft in the US. The ruling stated that Microsoft was attempting to establish a monopoly by forcing customers and business partners to use its software.

# Removing applications from your PC (cont.)

## Remove applications

**1** Click Change/Remove Programs.

**2** Scroll down the list and select the program you wish to remove.

**3** The information to the right tells you how frequently a program is used and how much disk space it occupies, though that information is not always accurate.

**4** Click the Change/Remove (sometimes labelled just Remove) to begin removing the program from your computer.

**5** A dialog will usually appear confirming the action, then a progress bar showing the removal and finally a confirmation that the program has been deleted. Just like an installation however this can vary greatly depending on the program, so you may well be asked to choose options along the way.

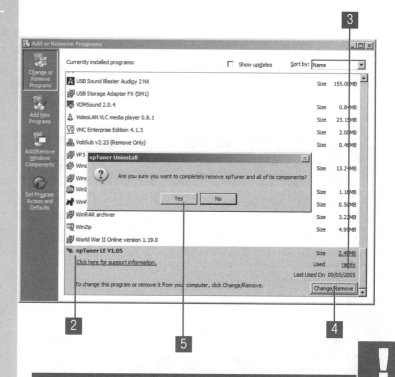

## Important

Sometimes the uninstall procedure will become corrupted and you'll be unable to remove a program through the Add/Remove programs option. In this situation you may be able to do it simply by locating the uninstall file in the program directory and running it; they're often named 'uninstall.exe' or some variation thereof, as it could be that Windows just cannot find the uninstall file itself. If this also refuses to work you can just delete the program folder. It would be a good idea however to move this into the recycle bin until you're sure you no longer need it, rather than completely deleting the files, just in case you encounter problems from Windows or other applications later on. Be aware that this will probably leave references to the application in the Windows Registry and if you want to completely remove these you will need to do it manually by searching the Registry.

**Windows Components Wizard**

**Windows Components**
You can add or remove components of Windows XP.

To add or remove a component, click the checkbox. A shaded box means that only part of the component will be installed. To see what's included in a component, click Details.

Components:

| | |
|---|---|
| ☐ Management and Monitoring Tools | 2.0 MB |
| ☐ Message Queuing | 0.0 MB |
| ☑ MSN Explorer | 13.2 MB |
| ☑ Networking Services | 0.3 MB |
| ☐ Other Network File and Print Services | 0.0 MB |

Description: Contains a variety of specialized, network-related services and protocols.

Total disk space required: 56.7 MB
Space available on disk: 92024.1 MB

Details...

< Back    Next >    Cancel

**1** Click the Add/Remove Windows Components button in Add/Remove Programs.

**2** This will display the Windows Components wizard, with various tools and features of Windows listed. Click on a listing to see a description.

**3** Boxes with no ticks signify a program or feature that is not installed.

**4** Boxes that are ticked with a white background indicate that feature is fully installed.

**5** Anything with a grey background indicates a feature that is partially installed.

**6** When available you can click Details to add and remove specific options from a component.

**7** Select an item to uninstall by removing the tick or install by ticking a box and using Details to select additional options and tools. Click Next and the actions will be carried out. Make sure you have your original Windows installation CD to hand as it may ask you to insert it.

**4**

# Changing default programs

**1** Click Set Program Access and Defaults.

**2** If you want to use only Microsoft products, select Microsoft Windows and click OK. To use non-Microsoft products, select that option. This will depend on programs being compatible with that function.

**3** The Custom option allows you to select exactly which programs are used. If an application is compatible with the Program Access function it will appear as an option in the list, otherwise you can use the Windows default or the current application.

**4** If you don't want a program to be available in Windows, uncheck the Enable Access box next it. This will remove links to the program on the desktop and start menu.

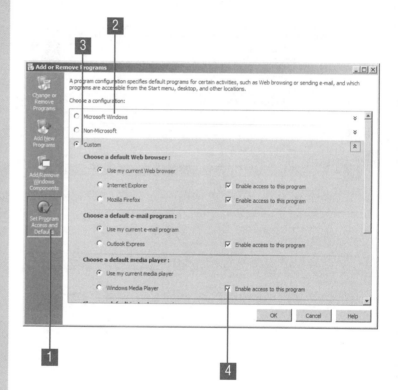

All common files in Windows will, or should, be associated with a program, meaning that if you open them they will always be viewed by that particular application. You can of course change this file association or just open a file once with an alternative program. All of this can be done very quickly and easily by opening the context menu on a file. You can also apply attributes, like making a file hidden or read-only, which will help stop them being overwritten or deleted because in most cases the computer should ask you before running any action on a read-only file.

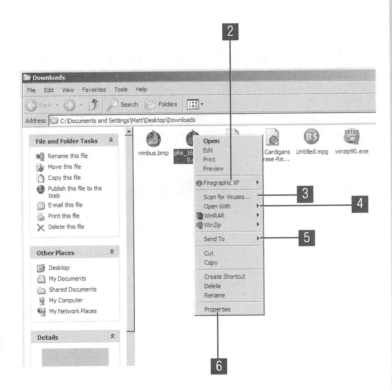

## Use file execution and view options

**1** Right-click on a file to bring up the context menu. The options that are shown will change depending on the file type.

**2** We've clicked on an image, so the context menu includes the relevant program associations for an image. In this case, the image browser Firegraphic XP has a menu with several options. It's also assigned as the default viewer for this file type, which is indicated by the file icon graphic.

**3** With a virus scanner installed you can instantly scan any file by choosing the appropriate option from the context menu. All virus scanners should include this function.

**4** Use the Open With menu to use a program other than the default application associated with that file.

**5** Use Send To when you wish to transfer the file to another part of your system or send it over the internet.

**6** You can view the file attributes by clicking the Properties option. This shows you information such as the file size, creation and modification dates and allows you to set options such as Read Only.

**4**

# Opening and modifying files (cont.)

## Run the file with the Open With menu

**1** Right-click on a file and select the Open With menu. This allows you to run the file with an alternative application from the list.

**2** Click Choose Program and you can select another program from your hard disk.

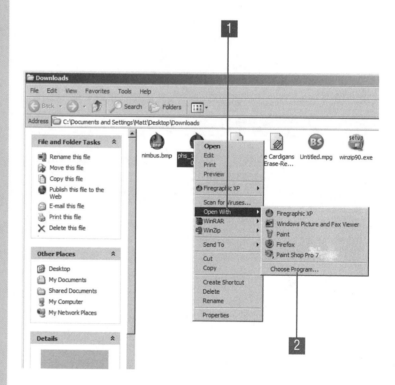

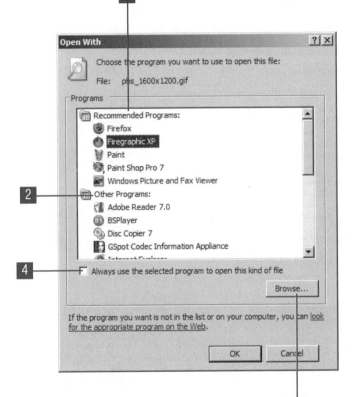

## Run the file with another application

**1** The Recommended Programs list shows programs that Windows already recognises.

**2** Other Programs shows other applications registered on your system, they may not necessarily be able to open the file.

**3** Click Browse to select another program from your hard disk.

**4** If you want to change the file association so that the file will always open with the program you choose, tick Always Use The Selected Program.

4

# Moving and copying files

Moving files around the system is incredibly simple, just a case of dragging and dropping them into new locations. You'll want to do this to keep your files organised but remember not to touch important system files and folders. If you attempt to move any system or read-only files Windows should usually warn you beforehand. Unless you know what you're doing it's best to leave them be.

Dragging and dropping files from one folder to another on the same drive will automatically move them. Doing it from one drive to another will copy the files.

## Copy and move files between folders

1. You can move a file by dragging and dropping it into another folder.

2. Or, right-click on a file and select Cut or Copy, then right-click in the new folder and choose Paste. Note that files copied into the same directory as the original will automatically have 'Copy of' added to the file name.

3. Move and copy groups of files by selecting them with the normal method and then using the Cut and Copy options.

4. You can also drag and drop with the right mouse button. When you release the button a context menu will appear with Copy, Move and Create Shortcut options. This is quicker than using the right-click Cut and Copy options.

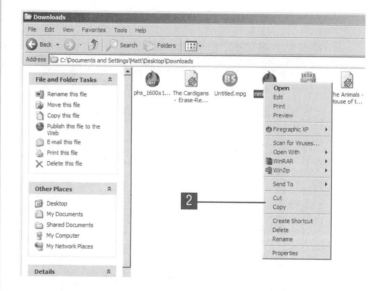

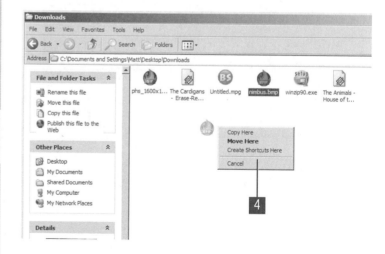

## Timesaver tip

Remember the shortcut keys for cutting and copying. Press Ctrl+X to cut, Ctrl+C to copy and Ctrl+V to paste. This works in most programs, not just copying files, e.g. you can cut and paste text in a word processor, or copy text off a website.

Once files are no longer required you should delete them from your system to free up hard disk space and reduce clutter. By default, Windows places deleted files in the Recycle Bin and this is something that many people don't learn until later on, when they've used up all the space and find several useless gigabytes sat in there. You can help your PC run smoothly by emptying the Bin on a regular basis or whenever it gets too full. Don't forget that it does actually have a purpose, though, because if you accidentally remove a file and place it in the Bin, it can be restored without any loss of data. If you're not bothered about this, you can delete files for good with a shortcut key or configure the Recycle Bin to always delete files immediately.

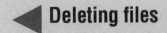

# Deleting files

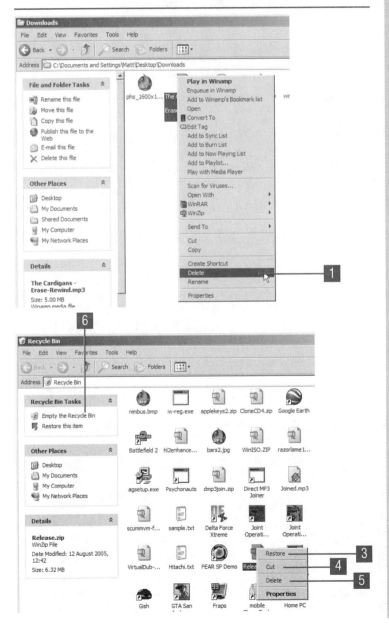

## Move files to the Recycle Bin

**1** By default, the Delete command will move files to the Recycle Bin. Select the file(s) and press the Delete key, or right-click and choose Delete, or drag and drop files into the Recycle Bin.

## Use the Recycle Bin

**2** Right-click on a file or group of files to bring up the options.

**3** Choose Restore to put the file back in its original location on your hard disk.

**4** Use Cut to move the file out of the Recycle Bin without restoring it to its original folder. You can then paste it to any location on your drive.

**5** Once you're sure you no longer need a file, choose the Delete option or hit Delete on your keyboard. This will remove it from your computer.

**6** You can clear the entire recycle bin by choosing the Empty Recycle Bin. This will delete every file at once.

## Timesaver tip

Hold down Shift and press Delete to bypass the Recycle Bin and delete a file straight away.

# Learning about Recycle Bin options

**1** Right-click on the Recycle Bin and choose Properties. Notice the Empty Recycle Bin option, which allows you to empty the bin without opening it.

**2** Check the Do Not Move Files to Recycle Bin option to delete files from your hard disk without them going to the recycle bin. Be careful when using this because once a file is deleted it can be difficult to recover.

**3** Move the slider to assign a percentage of each hard disks storage space to the recycle bin.

**4** Uncheck the Delete Confirm option to delete files immediately without a warning prompt. It's probably a good idea to leave this setting as is unless you have a very specific reason for it to be disabled.

**5** Use the Configure Drive independently option to configure the delete options for each drive, otherwise settings will be applied universally.

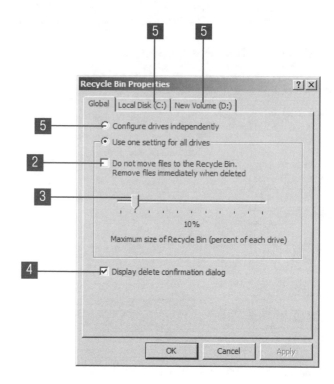

## Important

When you delete a file from Windows in the normal way, it isn't actually completely destroyed. What happens is that the operating system marks the space the file occupies as available, so that the next time data is written to the drive the old data could be overwritten. Even then, fragments of files can be retrieved using advanced techniques. From a security standpoint, this makes removing sensitive files a complete nightmare and experts will tell you that if data is of life or death importance, you should take the hard disk, dismantle it and then smash the pieces. Home users shouldn't need to go to those extremes however as there are a large number of file shredding applications which overwrite data multiple times and fill the gaps with junk information to make it harder to find. It won't stop dedicated police forensic units but if you sell your hard disk it will ensure that the new owner can't recover anything you've deleted. File shredders can be found on download sites or are included as part of packages like Symantec's Norton SystemWorks.

Creating new files and folders is easy, just use the right-click context menu and select the type of object you want. This is a quick way to create a new document or compressed zip file, for example, or a new folder. If you're handling lots of files, you can make life easy by using a bit of organisation and just creating folders to keep them grouped and organised.

◀
# Creating new files, folders and shortcuts

---

## Create a new file or folder

**1** Right-click to bring up the context menu, then go to New.

**2** On a clean installation of Windows, you will have the option to create a new folder, shortcut or several new file types, such as a text file.

**3** As you install applications, shortcuts for them will be added to the New menu. For example, we can create a new WinZip file without opening the WinZip application.

**4** Just click on the item you want to create and it will appear in the current folder. Type in a new name for the file or hit Enter to leave the default filename as it is.

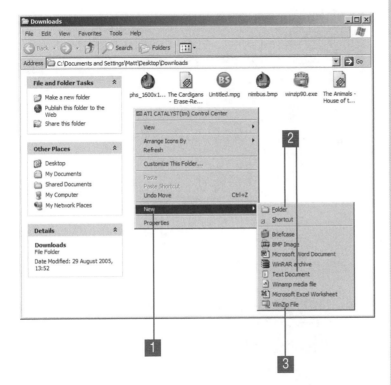

**4**

# Creating new files, folders and shortcuts (cont.)

## Make a shortcut

**1** Go to the New menu as before, but this time select New Shortcut.

**2** Click Browse and navigate to the location of the program you wish to shortcut.

**3** The full program location will appear in the box.

**4** Click Next.

**5** Now type in a name. By default it will use the name of the program file with an .EXE extension. Call it something that you'll easily recognise.

**6** Click Finish and the shortcut will be created.

### Timesaver tip

If you want to quickly rename a file or folder, click once to select it, then once again on the text and the name will become an input box. If the file extension is visible be careful not to delete that otherwise Windows may not be able to recognise the file. You can however change the extension if you wish.

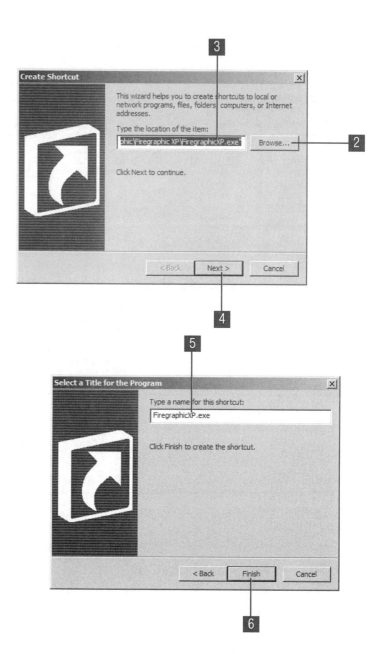

**3**

**Create Shortcut**

This wizard helps you to create shortcuts to local or network programs, files, folders, computers, or Internet addresses.

Type the location of the item:

`phic\Firegraphic XP\FiregraphicXP.exe`    Browse...    **2**

Click Next to continue.

< Back    Next >    Cancel

**4**

**5**

**Select a Title for the Program**

Type a name for this shortcut:

`FiregraphicXP.exe`

Click Finish to create the shortcut.

< Back    Finish    Cancel

**6**

Pretty soon, you'll find your hard disk filling up with files and folders. Unless you're Marvo the Memory Man or are extremely organised, finding one particular file can be a battle so it helps that Windows includes a built-in file search function. This is accessed from the Start menu and allows you to quickly find any file on your system. If you're looking for a picture, movie or audio file there is already a filter in place so you'll just need to enter a file name. You can also run a search for any file, use wildcards and apply advanced options such as date modified or file size. For most of us, the basic search is probably all we'll ever need but it's nice to know the extra options are there just in case.

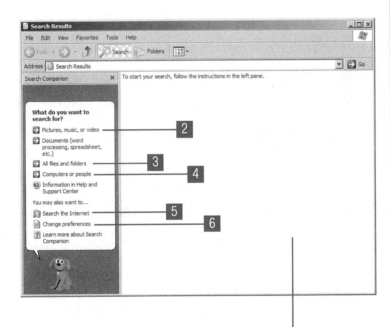

### Find files and folders on your PC

**1** Click Start, go to Search and choose Files and Folders to open the main search window.

**2** Select Pictures, Music and Video and Documents options to search for those file types only.

**3** All Files and Folders will do a system-wide scan without excluding any files.

**4** Computers and People can be used to find systems on a local network or names from your address book.

**5** Search the Internet will bring up an MSN search box.

**6** Change Preferences allows you to change the behaviour of the search function.

**7** Search results will be shown here.

**4**

**Timesaver tip**

Press Windows Key+F to instantly open the Search window.

# Searching your computer (cont.)

## Search for pictures, music or video

**1** Choose the Pictures, music or video option.

**2** Tick the boxes that match the type of items for which you wish to search.

**3** Type the filename into the search box, or as much of it as you can remember. Remember that partial information will often bring back more unwanted results, so try to be as exact as possible.

**4** Click Advanced Options.

**5** You can now search for text within the file, not just the file name itself. This is useful for documents but be careful about using common words as you'll get an unmanageable amount of hits.

**6** Use the Look In drop-down menu to select a specific location on your system to be searched.

**7** If you can remember the last time you modified the file or the approximate file size, enter this information to get more exact results.

**8** Further Advanced Options are available. You can choose to search hidden files or make the search case-sensitive.

**9** Click Search to start and once completed, the results will be displayed to the right.

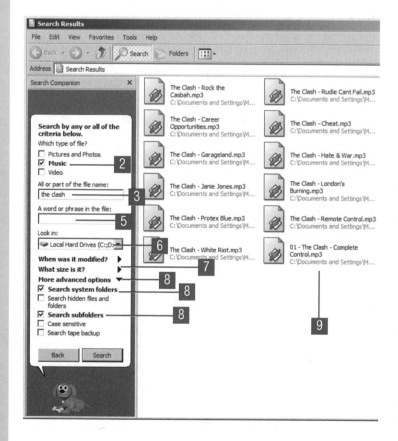

## Search all files and folders

1. In the Search window, select All Files and Folders.

2. As before, enter the file name into the search box. If you want to only search for files of a particular type, place a wildcard (*) in front of the file extension.

3. The same advanced options are available when you choose a File and Folder search.

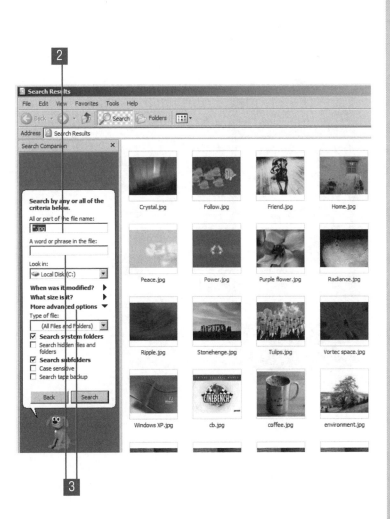

### Timesaver tip

When you run a search or anything involving large amounts of files, many programs will allow you to use wildcards to automatically include large groups of files. Placing a wildcard in front of an extension would cover every file of that type, while placing a wildcard in the extension would search for every file type with that exact name.

# Searching your computer (cont.)

## Change search options

**1** Click the Change Preferences option from the main Search window.

**2** Fed up with that animated doggy? Us too. Press Without an Animated Screen Character to banish him to the digital dog kennel.

**3** So you don't want the dog, what about choosing another irritating character to replace him? Click With a Different Character to select a new pal.

**4** Enable the Indexing Service. This makes searching faster, but your files will need to be checked and catalogued when the computer is idle.

**5** Change Files and Folders behaviour allows you to enable advanced search options so they will already be visible by default.

**6** Click Change Internet Search to select an alternative engine for searching the internet through the Search option.

**7** Disable the balloon tips that occasionally show to guide you.

**8** Enable or disable the auto-complete, which will finish words and file names for you as you type.

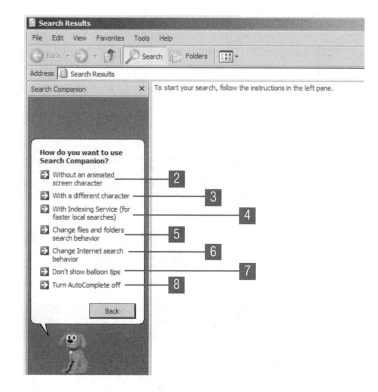

# Hardware

## Introduction

In the first chapter we gave you an overview of each component and its role, here we're going to show how you can perform a few of the most common upgrades. You're not going to be diving straight inside a brand new system the moment you get it, but eventually you'll want or need to open it up and make some changes to the innards. As your needs change and new software is released, you'll want more memory, hard disk space or graphical processing power, all of which is very easy to achieve by removing the old, plugging in the new and (sometimes) installing new drivers. Performing simple upgrades yourself takes very little time and can save you money where computer stores would charge for labour on top of parts, for a job that could take less than a few minutes. Modern systems are, in general, incredibly easy to build and maintain once you've got compatible parts, slotting together like expensive, electronic building blocks. You do need to be careful when handling components as they can be easily damaged by rough treatment and static diskharge, but this is avoided simply by following a few basic safety rules. Once you've learnt the basics you could even start thinking about building your next system, which gives you total control over the quality of the hardware used, saves money and is incredibly satisfying once your new home-made PC is up and running.

## What you'll do

**Install a new graphics card**

**Change your graphics card settings**

**Upgrade your memory**

**Install a new hard disk**

**Create multiple partitions**

**Install a new CD or DVD drive**

**Manage your hardware with Device Manager**

# Installing a new graphics card

If you're planning on just using your PC for office tasks, it's unlikely you'll ever need to touch the graphics card. If however you want to dabble in video or graphics editing or gaming then a new card is a possibility or even a necessity, especially if your system only came with a weak onboard or budget model. Fitting a card is usually pain-free, with the only problems coming from fiddly slot catches or outdated drivers. One very important thing you must check however is that any new card you buy is compatible with your motherboard. Newer motherboards use the new PCI-express interface standard while slightly older systems take AGP. Neither is compatible with the other, so check that you don't buy a PCI-express card for your AGP system. You'll also need to check that your power supply unit is properly equipped to handle the card. The very latest models use a great deal of power so a good 400W power supply is recommended, but you also need to ensure that you have a spare Molex power cable or, in the case of PCI-express cards, a six-pin PCI-e power connecter. Don't rush out to buy a new PSU if yours doesn't have the six-pin connection though, because most cards should include an adapter and if not, they can be purchased for a small amount from computer suppliers.

## Important

If you've got an on-board graphics card (you'll know, because the monitor port will be alongside the other connections on the back of the motherboard and there'll be no graphics card in an expansion slot) you will need to disable this to use your new card. Enter your PCs BIOS (usually done by hitting the Del key when the PC first starts, though the methods can vary – consult your mother-board manual) then find the Integrated Peripherals section. There you should find an entry for on-board graphics. Disable it completely, then save and exit.

## Jargon buster

**AGP** – Accelerated Graphics Port, based on the PCI interface, AGP was developed exclusively for graphics cards, replacing the general-use PCI slot. It's now being phased out in favour of PCI-express, but AGP cards are still being manufactured because of the abundance of AGP systems.

**Anti-static bag** – components are usually shipped in grey plastic bags that have been treated to protect against static damage. It's a good idea to hold on to these as they may come in useful when upgrading.

**BIOS** – Basic Input Output System, the software that enables basic functionality of hardware on all systems, whether they have an operating system or not, and allows you to configure hardware settings. The BIOS is stored on a Read-Only Memory (ROM) chip on the motherboard, so will always be available even if the hard disk crashes. You can access your BIOS by hitting the assigned key when your system starts, which is usually Delete.

**PCI** – Peripheral Component Interconnect, the most common type of interface found on PC systems now, it still appears on the very latest PCI-express boards to support expansion hardware like sound cards, which have yet to switch to using PCI-express.

**PCI-Express** – the 'sequel' to PCI and AGP interfaces, PCI-express offers a (potentially) huge increase in bandwidth. Newer motherboards include one or two PCI-e slots specifically for graphics cards and several more for additional expansion cards, alongside a couple of standard PCI slots.

5

Empty graphics card slot

### Remove the previous card

1  Before you do anything else, go into Add/Remove programs and uninstall your current graphics card drivers. Shut down the system once that is finished.

2  If you already have a graphics card in the AGP or PCI-express slot, you'll obviously need to remove it first.

3  If the card has an extra power cable attached, carefully unplug this. The 6-pin PCI-express power connectors have a small catch that you'll need to press down on to release them.

4  The card bracket will be secured to the case in some way, usually with a screw though sometimes there is a tool-free mechanism. Release this so the card is loosened.

5  You'll now need to flick the slot catch which holds the card in place. Just press down on it until the back of the card pushes upwards. Some boards may have a slightly different mechanism, like a sliding catch, but these are quite rare.

6  Carefully lift the card out the slot and place it somewhere safe, preferably in an anti-static bag within a sturdy box.

5

# Installing a new graphics card (cont.)

## Install the new card

1. Simply put, you need to do the opposite of the previous steps. First make sure the slot catch is pushed all the way back.

2. Carefully and gently push the new card into the slot. Make sure that the lower part of the bracket slips between the back of the case and the motherboard and doesn't get caught.

3. Once the card is in the correct position, push firmly down on it until the slot catch clicks into place. Check that it's properly seated; it should be able to wiggle from side to side but not lift at the back.

4. Now secure the bracket to the case. Your card should be firmly fixed into place so that there's no movement and no possible chance of it coming loose when you plug in the monitor.

5. If additional power is required, use the appropriate power connection on the rear of the card, Molex for AGP and six-pin for PCI-express.

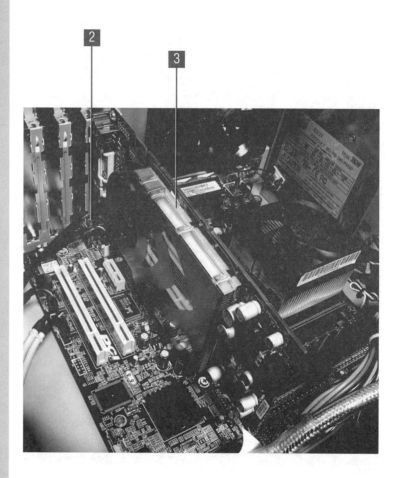

## Important

Hardware is extremely sensitive to static; you won't even know you've killed that brand new RAM module until your system refuses to start, so always take precautions when handling components. Use an anti-static wristband (available from computer stores) or if that's not possible, regularly touch a grounded metal object to diskharge any static build-up. Avoid working on carpet; lino or wooden floors are preferable. RAM, CPUs and graphics cards are particularly sensitive and also some of the most expensive parts, so always exercise extreme caution when handling these components.

## Installing the graphics card drivers

3

---

Customer Care Home | Knowledgebase | My Support                    Welcome Guest. Sign in | Exit
Knowledge Base | Troubleshooter

### Knowledge Base
ATI Customer Care > Drivers and Software > Windows XP > RADEON >

**CATALYST 5.8 Windows XP - Driver Download**

related topics

CATALYST CREW
Feedback

HYDRAVISION - For
RADEON and Mobile ATI
Products

ATI Multimedia Center 9.08

ATI Trade Up Program
✓ Buy a new ATI graphics card
✓ Send us your old graphics card
✓ Get USD$50 for your old graphics card

**Instructions:**
- For details on this driver, including resolved issues, please review the RELEASE NOTES.
- Installing a new driver is only recommended if you are having issues with your ATI product.

**Notes:**
- ATI recommends Windows XP Service Pack 2 or higher to be installed.
- You must have Microsoft .NET Framework installed prior to downloading and installing the CATALYST Control Center
- The CATALYST Uninstaller is an optional download. We recommend using this utility to uninstall any previously installed CATALYST drivers prior to installation.
- CATALYST Control Center is available in a bundle supporting English, French, German, Japanese, Simplified Chinese and Spanish. Additional languages will be available in future updates.

topic information

Topic #: 737-640
Date Created: 1/20/2005
Modified: 8/17/2005
Times Viewed: 11855112

Print Topic
Email Topic
Back

| Connection Speed | CATALYST Component | Download Link | File Size (KB/MB) | Date Posted | Additional Info and components |
|---|---|---|---|---|---|
| High Speed (Cable / DSL) | With Control Panel | Download 1 of 1 | 25.2 | 08/17/05 | Display and WDM Drivers included in this bundle |
| | With CATALYST Control Center | Download 1 of 1 | 32.8 | 08/17/05 | Display and WDM Drivers included in this bundle |

1. Once you reboot with your new card you will need to install the drivers in order for it to work properly. Windows will display – but only in a lower resolution.

2. Windows will tell you it has found new hardware, click cancel, we don't want it to install any other software.

3. If you have a driver CD, insert that and it will start automatically, just follow the prompts to install. Otherwise, you will need to download the drivers off the manufacturer's website. NVIDIA card owners should go to www.nvidia.com while ATi's site is www.ati.com.

4. Run the install routines and follow the installation steps, they are straightforward and once finished will reboot your system.

### Important

You should check regularly to see that your graphics card drivers are up-to-date, since newer versions will offer improved performance, stability and features.

5

# Changing your graphics card settings

Both NVIDIA and ATi, manufacturers of the most popular graphics cards, provide numerous options for their cards with the driver software. Although you do not need to change these settings to use the card, they do offer an extra level of control. We're going to take a look at ATi's Catalyst Control Center as an example, but the software from both companies is accessed in the same way and offers a similar level of customisation.

## Open the graphics card controls

**1** Right-click on your desktop and choose Properties or, if you have Catalyst Control Center installed, choose the ATi Catalyst Control Center option.

**2** If you chose Properties, click the Settings tab and then Advanced.

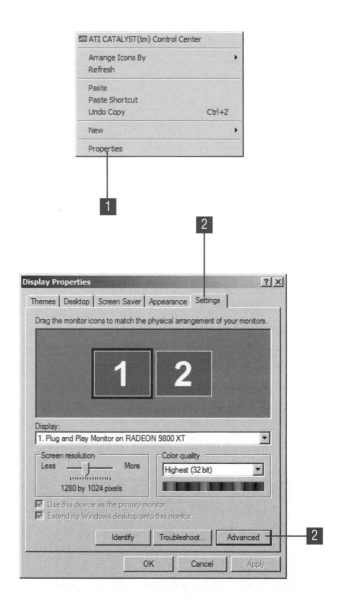

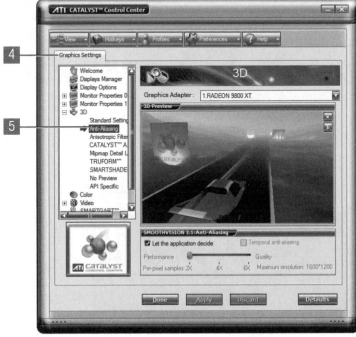

# Changing your graphics card settings (cont.)

## Use the Control Center

1 This demo shows you a preview of the changes you make.

2 By default the software is running in basic mode, use the slider to change the quality or performance of the visuals.

3 Use the View button to switch to advanced and bring up a menu tree with a complete break-down of the options available.

4 Within advanced you have many other settings, not just covering 3D performance but also monitor settings, color controls and video display.

5 Click on an entry in the tree to see the available options. Some settings, such as Anti-Aliasing, are best left on their default configuration unless you know precisely what you're doing.

5

# Upgrading your memory

Certainly one of the easiest upgrades you can perform, the biggest hurdles you've got when upgrading memory is ensuring you buy the correct type. With SDRAM, DDR, DDR2, ECC, Non-ECC and latency ratings to deal with, it can become incredibly confusing. For current systems, DDR-400 RAM is used with AMD processors and DDR2 is required for the new Intel CPUs. You can use your motherboard manual to see what RAM is used, check the sticker on your current RAM modules or contact the supplier of your PC to find out.

## Remove the old memory

1. Locate the two catches on either end of the RAM slot and push them down. The module will rise out of the slot, gently lift it out and place it in an anti-static bag for safe-keeping.

## Jargon buster

**AMD** – Advanced Micro Devices, Intel's only real competitor in the CPU market is AMD, who make the extremely popular Athlon and Athlon 64 series of processors.

**DDR-RAM** – Double Data Rate RAM, the follow-up to SDRAM, this type of memory is currently used in AMD systems.

**DDR-2** – the successor to DDR-RAM. Supposedly faster though there's actually little difference between the two types of memory. DDR-2 is currently used only in Intel systems.

**Intel** – the largest manufacturer of central processing units in the world. The US giant had a monopoly on the CPU market until AMD introduced the Athlon series processor.

## Important

RAM is incredibly sensitive to static. When handling it take care not to touch the gold contacts or chips, hold it by the edges whenever possible and take the usual precautions against static build-up.

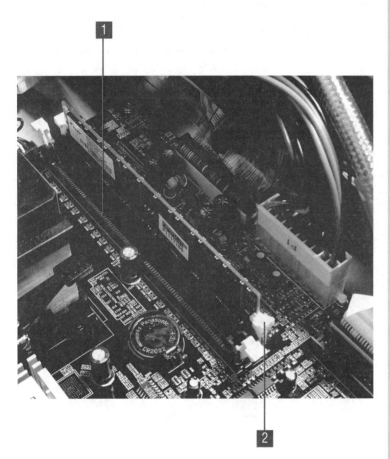

## Insert the new memory

1 Line up the notches in the RAM modules with the slots on the motherboard and carefully place them.

2 Once you're sure that they're in the right position, push firmly until the catches either end click into place. It shouldn't require much force, so if you feel a lot of resistance double-check that the modules are definitely lined up properly.

3 That's it! Boot up your system and watch during the POST as the memory is counted and checked. No drivers are needed.

### Jargon buster

**POST** – Power On Self-Test, the check that every computer runs when it first powers up, to ensure that all necessary hardware is present and correct.

5

### Important

If you're buying two or more RAM modules, for example two 512 MB sticks to make 1 GB, you must make sure that they are both the same type and from the same manufacturer. RAM is notoriously finicky and doesn't play well with other modules, so even if you got two sticks that had the same speed rating they may not work properly if they were made by different companies. The safest bet is to buy a matched-pair set, which guarantees you compatibility.

# Installing a new hard disk

Unlike memory and graphics cards, there's a little more to fitting a hard disk. Although physically installing it is usually very easy, as simple to do as a new DVD drive, you must then format and configure the hard disk so that it's ready for use. If you're fitting it as a secondary drive, this is simpler as it will just need formatting. If you're going to be installing Windows and you're using a serial ATA hard disk, however, things get a little more complex. You will need to use a floppy disk containing the drivers for the HDD (hard disk drive) so Windows can recognise it.

## Remove the old drive

**1** We're going to assume you've backed up all your vital data to an external drive. You have, right?

**2** Pop open your PC case and locate the drive bays holding the hard disk(s). Obviously, if you want to keep your current drive, you can skip this task entirely.

**3** Unplug the power and data cables. These can be quite stiff so gently wiggle them from side to side until they loosen.

**4** It used to be that all hard disks and other components were secured with screws – nowadays there's a good chance you have some kind of tool-less system, which makes life a great deal easier as the drives will usually just slide in and out. If they're screwed in, remove the screws and gently slide the drive from its bay. You may need to remove both side panels from your PC to get to screws on the other side.

## For your information

With the advent of serial ATA (SATA) drives, we no longer need to worry about master and slave configurations. SATA drives are hooked up to individual numbered connections on the board and do not share cables. Drive 0 is the first, 1 the second and so on.

## Change the jumper settings

1  If you're fitting an IDE hard disk (the type with big fat ribbon cables) then you'll probably need to change the jumper settings. These tell the system what role the drive plays, whether it is the primary drive (master) or secondary (slave). SATA drive users can skip this entirely.

2  Look on the end of your hard disk – next to the power and data cable connections will be a small row of pins with a tiny piece of plastic covering two of them. This is the jumper.

3  On top of the drive will be a label showing the jumper setting. Pull the jumper plug out with tweezers (or long nails) and move it so that it covers the pins specified by the label for the setting you require. Master is usually the default.

## Jargon buster

**IDE** – Intelligent Drive Electronics or Integrated Drive Electronics, an interface used on CD/DVD drives and hard disks, where the controlling electronics are on the device itself. Also referred to as EIDE, ATA or PATA.

**Jumpers** – a circuit bridge that allows the user to adjust the settings of a device by covering the jumper pins with a plastic plug.

**SATA** – Serial Advanced Technology Attachment, introduced to replace the ageing IDE interface. In addition to offering significant speed increases over IDE, SATA uses smaller cables, which helps with cable management and airflow inside the case.

# Installing a new hard disk (cont.)

## Fit the new hard disk

**1** Take your new hard disk and slot it into a space in the drive bay. If you have a tool-less system you may need to clip on a bracket first so that it rides along the rails and clicks into place.

**2** If your drives need to be screwed in, hold them in place and attach screws to either side of the drive bay. You can do it on one side only but it's less secure and may vibrate slightly, causing an irritating buzzing noise.

**3** Hook up the power and data cables. If the drive is a replacement you can use the same cable that was attached to your old drive, otherwise you'll need to plug a new cable into your motherboard.

**4** Seal up your PC and switch it on!

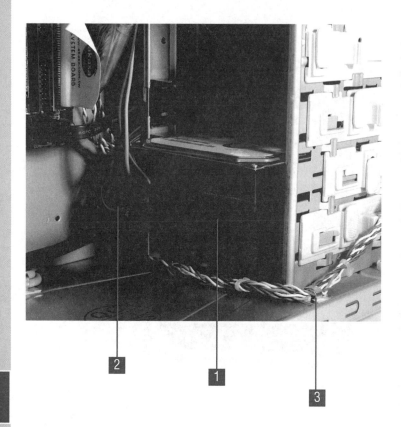

## Important

If you're attaching a secondary IDE drive, it will need to be set as master or slave depending on where it's going. If you put it on the same cable as your current primary drive or a CD/DVD drive, set it as slave. If it's going on its own on the secondary IDE connection, use the master jumper setting.

## Important

If you're planning a fresh install of Windows onto a Serial ATA hard disk, you'll need to check you have a copy of the SATA drivers on a floppy disk. The installation routine cannot detect SATA drives so when you begin you'll be prompted to hit F6 to select drivers for other devices. When asked, insert the SATA driver disk so Windows can see your hard disk.

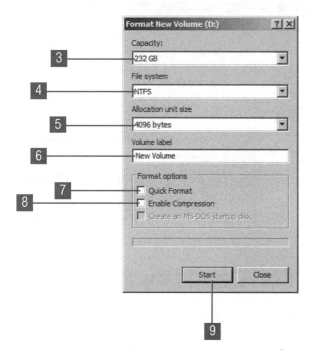

## Set up your new drive

**1** When you boot your system, you should see the extra drive listed during the POST. After this, one of two things will happen. Either your system will boot as normal or it will complain that no operating system has been found. If you're installing a fresh drive, dig out those rescue or Windows disks and install the operating system.

**2** Assuming that you're just fitting a secondary drive, you'll want to get into Windows and format it. Open up My Computer and see if the drive is listed, if so, right-click and choose Format.

**3** Capacity tells you the storage space of your hard disk.

**4** Select a file system. Our only option here is NTFS, which is preferable for Windows XP systems anyway.

**5** Leave the allocation size at the default setting.

**6** Type a name for your drive in the volume label box, this is optional.

**7** Quick Format will just do a quick sweep of the drive, use it if you just want to quickly clear one of your drives. If you're formatting a new disk don't select this.

**8** Enabling compression will allow you to compress files and folders to save space.

**9** Click Start to begin formatting. The time this takes will vary depending on the size of the drive.

## Jargon buster

**FAT32** – File Allocation Table 32, the 32-bit file system available since Windows 95, which supports hard disks of up to 2 terabytes in size.

**NTFS** – NT File System, used by Windows NT and later, NTFS offers several advantages over FAT32 such as greater reliability and file and folder security.

**5**

# Using Disk Management

## Timesaver tip

When you plug in a new external drive you may also find that is not listed either. If that happens, follow the steps for enabling and formatting a new hard disk.

1 In the last steps we showed you how to set up a drive in Windows, but what if your hard disk isn't even showing in My Computer when you restart? This is easily fixed with Disk Management.

2 To bring up Disk Management, either right-click on My Computer and select Manage or go to Start, Run and type compmgmt.msc then hit OK. Click Disk Management from the menu tree.

3 If your new drive appears with a black bar and says 'Unallocated', like our example, it means that it needs to be partitioned and formatted before use. Right-click and choose New Partition.

4 Follow the New Partition wizard. Leave the default options as they are and don't change them unless you have a specific reason.

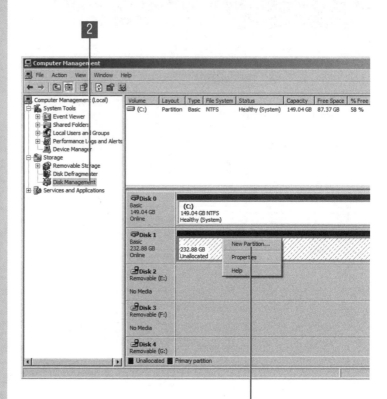

## Jargon buster

**Partition** – to divide a hard disk into several individual parts. The operating system then sees each drive partition as a separate disk, as if you had multiple physical hard disks installed.

# Changing drive settings

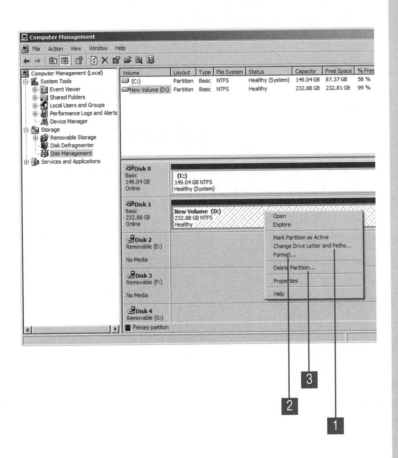

1. Now that your drive is partitioned and formatted, right-click on a disk in Disk Management to bring up a list of options. You can change the drive letter and related file paths, but be aware that this may result in some programs not working if they're unable to find files.

2. Clicking Format brings up the same drive formatting options as we looked at previously.

3. If you want to start again, choose delete partition. The drive will no longer be visible in My Computer.

# Creating multiple partitions

Partitioning your disk – dividing the file space into multiple virtual drives – can help keep your data organised and also offers a quick 'n' dirty backup solution. Split a disk in two and you can format and wipe the other while safely storing data on the second half of it. Partitions are easily created using the Disk Management tool.

**1** Back up all the data you want to keep, then right-click in Disk Management and choose Delete partition. The hard disk will be wiped clean and all current settings removed.

**2** The drive will now say 'Unallocated'. Right-click and select New Partition.

**3** Follow the New Partition wizard, clicking the default options until it asks you to choose a file size.

**4** By default it will select the full capacity of the hard disk but we're going to enter our own file size, 100,000 MB (100 GB) in this case.

**5** Complete the New Partition wizard, formatting the drive and selecting other options in the usual manner.

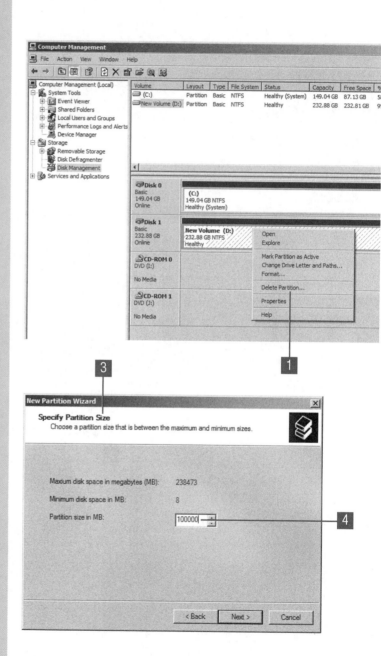

## Create additional partitions

6 You'll be taken back to the Disk Management tool, but this time you'll see that rather than one disk, you now have two.

7 The remaining drive space can be formatted or partitioned by creating a new partition.

## Important

Do not partition your C: drive or any other disk containing an operating system, as it will wipe the data it contains. If you need to partition a hard disk that's in use you'll need to use a specialised tool like Norton PartitionMagic. It's recommended that you use this tool if you regularly partition your hard drives as it makes the process much easier and safer.

5

# Installing a new CD or DVD drive

If you don't already have a DVD writer of some description, there's little excuse now that prices are so low. Good quality, brand name burners can be found for £40 or even less, and as well as allowing you to easily back up your system they'll also let you create your own DVD video disks. Installing a new optical drive is a similar procedure to fitting a hard disk, but with a lot less messing about afterwards, since there's no need to format or partition a DVD drive. Most drives, even now, are IDE although models using the SATA interface are slowly coming on sale. Like hard disks IDE optical drives must be configured for master or slave, they can also share a cable with a hard disk.

## Remove the current drive

1 Pull out the power and data cables from the drive.

2 Locate the screws or mechanism holding the drive in place and remove them.

3 Slide the drive out from the front of your case.

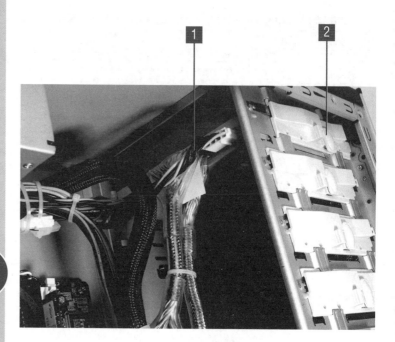

### For your information

DVD drives, like home DVD players, include region-locking features. However, unlike standalone players you can select which region your drive uses, since you get an average of five chances to select an alternate region, with the final region being the one you're stuck with permanently. Don't worry if your drive does get stuck on a region though, there are fixes. There are many applications available for disabling region settings, the most popular of which is DVD Region Free.

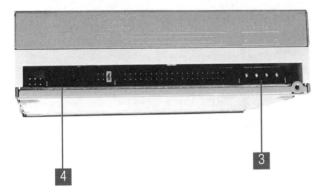

# Installing a new CD or DVD drive (cont.)

### Install the new drive

1. Slide the drive into the gap from the front of the case. If you're adding a second drive, you'll need to pop out a faceplate and possibly twist off the metal plate behind that. Don't forget to set the Master/Slave configuration in the same way as a hard disk.

2. Line up the holes on the side of the drive with those on the drive cage and screw the drive down. As with a hard disk, it's a good idea to do this on both sides of the cage, especially since optical drives can make a real racket as they spin.

3. Connect up the power and data cables.

4. Optical drives also have CD-audio outputs, if you have a cable for this going into your soundcard or onboard sound then you should also plug in the 'CD-OUT' connector.

5. Once the drive is connected, start your system. It will automatically be detected and no software is needed. You may, however, need to reinstall any disk burning software so it can detect the new drive.

5

# Managing your hardware with Device Manager

Device Manager is the central point in Windows for monitoring your hardware. It contains the details of every component and attached peripheral with options for managing each one. If you encounter problems with an item of hardware, you can use the Device Manager to uninstall and reinstall the device, roll back the driver to a previous version or temporarily disable the hardware.

## Use Device Manager

**1** Go to Control Panel and double-click System.

**2** In System, click the Hardware tab, then Device Manager.

**3** Click the + button next to each item in the tree to expand the view and see further details on the hardware.

**4** Right-click on an item of hardware to view the available options.

**5** Click Update Driver to have Windows search for a newer version of the driver software. It's generally better to find newer drivers for yourself, though.

**6** Click Disable to switch off the device. It will stay off until activated again and will not be detected by Windows when you restart.

**7** Click Uninstall to completely remove the hardware from Windows. If you reboot and the hardware is still present in your computer, Windows will detect it and attempt to set it up again.

**8** Scan For Hardware Changes can be used to find hardware after you've uninstalled it.

**9** Click Properties to bring up more information about the selected hardware device.

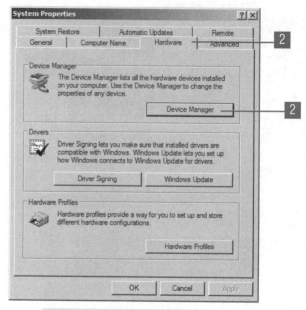

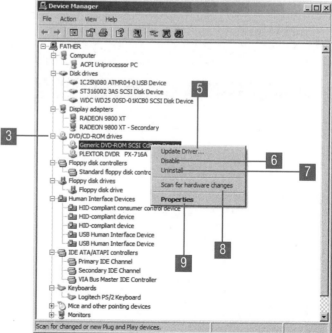

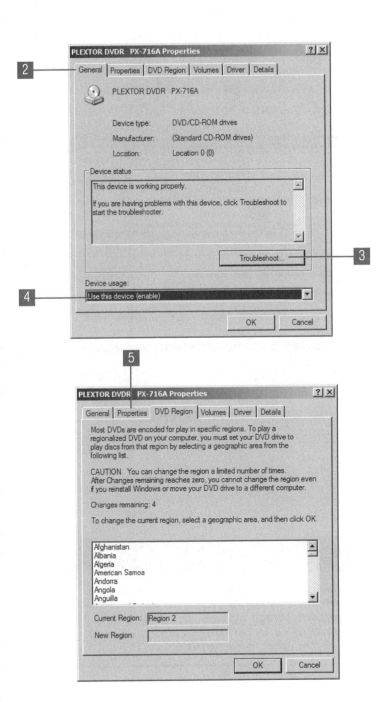

## Learn about hardware properties

1. The Properties of each device varies wildly, with some having several options and others with little to no information.

2. In the General tab you'll find information about the current status of the device.

3. The Troubleshoot button opens Windows help, with specific questions about your device. Unfortunately, it's not that useful in most situations.

4. You can disable the hardware with the Device Usage drop-down box.

5. Click the Properties tab. For an optical drive, the Properties will allow us to change the CD player volume and enable/disable digital CD audio.

5

# Managing your hardware with Device Manager (cont.)

**6** One unique option of DVD drives is the ability to select another region. Click the Region tab, choose a country from the list and click OK to set that region.

**7** The Changes Remaining number tells you how many times you're allowed to set the region before it's locked.

**8** The Driver tab is available in the properties for much of the hardware and gives you information about the currently installed driver software.

**9** Click Update Driver to search online for a newer version.

**10** Roll Back Driver will restore your system to use the previously installed driver.

**11** Uninstall will remove the driver and require re-installation of the hardware device.

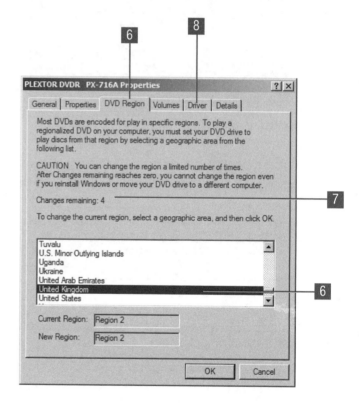

## For your information

Devices that are not functioning correctly will be flagged with warning icons and their menu view already expanded when you open Device Manager. This will include hardware that is disabled or not installed. You can then right-click it as normal and take the appropriate action to resolve the problem.

# Internet

## Introduction

Like or not, the internet is now an integral part of the modern computing experience, you're missing out on half the fun if you've got a PC and you're not online. Assuming you've got antivirus and a firewall (see Chapter 3 for more information) getting on the net is easy and safe. If you just want to send some email and browse the web, a 56 k dial-up connection is the cheapest method, but to get the most out of it you'll want to be looking at an ADSL or cable broadband connection. There are hundreds of different services offering speeds from 256 k right up to 10 MB and beyond, with prices that vary from as little as £9.99 per month. Two things to watch out for though are contract length and bandwidth limits. Some companies will give you a monthly contract, so you can cancel without any penalty, while annual contracts will incur a charge if you cancel. Bandwidth limits are imposed to stop heavy users taking all the resources. You will be given an allowance, in GB transferred per month. Going over that will either result in your speed being reduced or a charge for the additional data. If you're planning on heavy use, get a service without any limit. We're going to look at web browsing, email and instant messaging in this chapter. Apart from Messenger, we've ignored the usual Microsoft products, simply because their popularity and insecurity can be a danger to new users. Alternatives such as Firefox have more features and better security than the ubiquitous Internet Explorer.

### Jargon buster

**Bandwidth** – the amount of data that can be transmitted within a certain amount of time. For internet connections, this is bps, bytes per second.

**Email** – electronic mail, messages sent over an electronic network, stored in a server until the recipient reads them.

**Instant Messaging** – a method of communication that creates a private chat room between yourself and at least one other person. Instant Messaging can be used to send text or files.

## What you'll do

**Install the web browser Firefox**

**Configure Firefox**

**Use Firefox Extensions**

**Browse the web with Firefox**

**Manage bookmarks**

**Setup an email account**

**Use Fastmail**

**Send email**

**Configure MSN Messenger**

**Chat over Instant Messaging**

**Send and receive files**

# Installing the web browser Firefox

Since 1999, Internet Explorer has been the dominant web browser with over 90% of the market share, largely because it's bundled with Windows. However, the past few years have seen a backlash against Internet Explorer fuelled by countless security holes that left PCs wide open to attack from viruses, spyware and malicious websites. Mozilla, the open-source offshoot of Netscape, has taken advantage of the situation, first releasing the fully-featured Mozilla web browser and, more recently, its slimmed-down sibling Firefox. The latter has become hugely popular thanks to its security, speed and customisation options, which is why we're using it here. This totally free application is not only safer but also makes browsing the web a smoother, more enjoyable experience.

1 Pop over to www.firefox.com and enter the website.

2 Click the Download link and save the installation file to your hard disk.

3 Double-click the Firefox installation file.

## For your information

As well as Internet Explorer and Firefox, there are many other alternative web browsers for you to choose. Netscape (www.netscape.com) is still around, but is a modified version of the Gecko engine that Firefox is built upon. The next most popular browser after Internet Explorer and Firefox is Opera (www.opera.com), which offers similar compatibility to Firefox but boasts an extensive range of features. There's also a slew of browsers based upon Internet Explorer, some free and some shareware, which add features like tabbed browsing and pop-up blocking to the worlds number 1 browser.

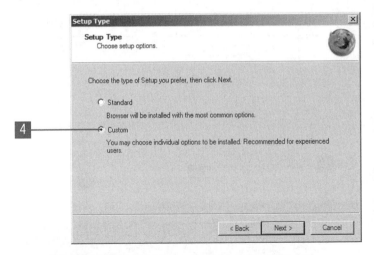

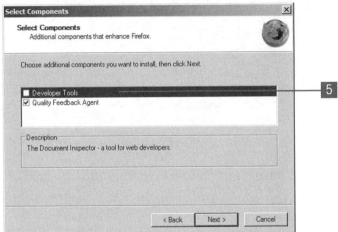

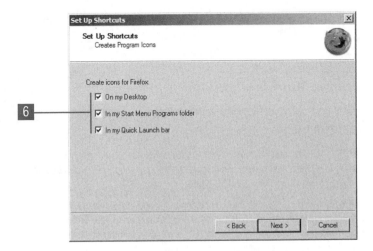

**4** Click through the license agreement and select Standard or Custom installation. We'll go with custom, but standard just uses the default installation options.

**5** Choose whether you want to install the Developer Tools and Quality Feedback Agent. Unless you're a web developer the tools will be useless, but Quality Feedback Agent allows you to send in bug reports when Firefox crashes, which can assist the development team.

**6** Check or uncheck the boxes to choose where shortcut icons will be placed.

# Configuring Firefox

## Use General Options

**1** Open the Tools menu on the toolbar and click Options.

**2** The General tab contains miscellaneous options for the browser.

**3** You can change the default home page, which is what appears when each browser opens and when you click the home button on the browser toolbar.

**4** Select an alternative color scheme for Firefox.

**5** Choose a language.

**6** Click the default browser box and Firefox will check to see if it's still the default browser. If not, it will ask if you want to change or keep the current browser.

**7** Click Connection Settings if you need to set a **proxy** connection for web, **FTP** and other connection types. Unless you know exactly what you need to change in here it's unlikely you'll ever use this menu.

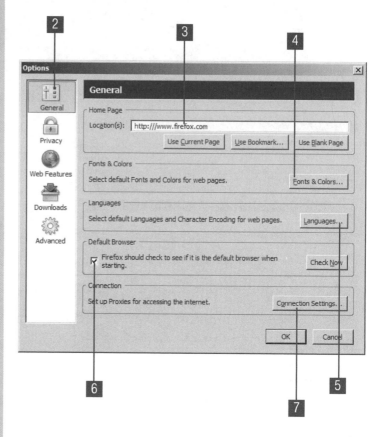

## Jargon buster

**FTP** – File Transfer Protocol, a method for downloading and uploading files to another system over a network. If you're creating a webpage you will usually have to login via FTP to upload the files.

**Proxy server** – sits between your computer and the server you're trying to access, so the proxy receives the data and sends it on to you. Proxies are often used as a method of anonymously browsing the internet, since the rest of the net sees the proxy details and not yours.

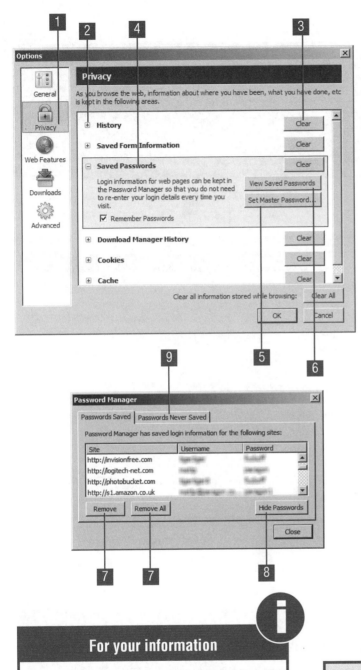

## Change privacy settings

**1** Use the Privacy tab to manage stored passwords, cookies and other data.

**2** Click the plus buttons to view additional options in each category.

**3** The Clear button next to each category will wipe stored information.

**4** The Saved Passwords options allow you to control website passwords you've saved. You can stop Firefox from saving passwords by clearing the Remember Passwords box.

**5** Click Set Master Password to protect your saved password data.

**6** View Saved Passwords will show you the saved usernames and passwords.

**7** Click Remove and Remove All to delete stored password information.

**8** Click Show Passwords to display the passwords. If the Master Password is enabled you will need to enter it. Click Hide Passwords to hide them again.

**9** The Passwords Never Saved tab displays sites for which you've chosen to never save passwords. The prompt for saving or not saving will appear when you login into a new site.

### For your information

Microsoft is currently working on Internet Explorer 7, which they hope will challenge Firefox and others by introducing features like **pop-up** blocking and tabbed browsing. At the time of writing it's currently in the beta stage, but if you do use Iinternet Explorer it will almost certainly be worth upgrading when the final version becomes available.

### Jargon buster

**Pop-up** – a window that pops up uninvited, usually for advertising. They can be very irritating and without a blocker your system can be flooded. There are also pop-unders, which appear underneath your browser.

6

# Configuring Firefox (cont.)

## The Web Features options

**1** Disable the block pop-up option to stop Firefox from suppressing pop-up windows.

**2** Check the Allow sites to install software option and websites will be able to install software in your browser. For security reasons it's best to leave this switched off.

**3** Click the Allowed Sites buttons to manage the sites that you've allowed to open pop-ups and run software. You should add sites you regularly visit to save allowing a pop-up each time.

**4** Uncheck Load Images to switch off images in Firefox.

**5** Setting sites in the Exceptions for images allows you to load images from a site when it's blocked. If you don't want to block all images, set specific sites to be blocked in here.

**6** Disabling Java and Javascript will stop websites that use these features from working. Javascript in particular can be a security vulnerability so you may want to keep it switched off until needed.

**7** The Advanced options tell Firefox what Javascript applications are allowed to do, this includes resizing and moving windows.

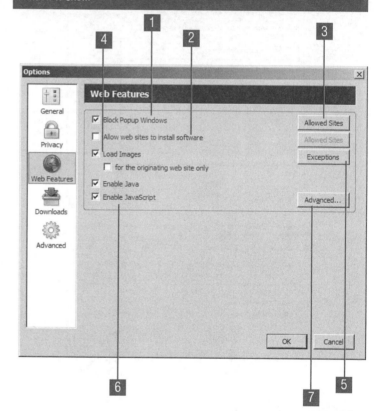

## Jargon buster

**Java** – a programming language created by Sun Microsystems and widely used in websites for features like chat rooms and games, through small Java programs called Applets. Also common on mobile phones.

**Javascript** – not related to Java, a scripting language created by Netscape for the production of interactive websites. It is supported by most modern web browsers.

## Download options

**Options** [×]

**Downloads**

General

**Download Folder**

[1]

○ Ask me where to save every file

● Save all files to this folder: [ Desktop ▼ ] [ Show Folder ]

Privacy

**Download Manager**

[2]

☑ Show Download Manager window when a download begins.

  ☑ Close the Download Manager when all downloads are complete.

Web Features

**File Types**

Automatically perform the associated action with each of the following file types:

Downloads

Advanced

[ Change Action... ] [ Remove ] [ Plug-Ins... ]

[3] [3]

[ OK ] [ Cancel ]

[1] Select where you want downloaded files saved, choose Ask Me to have Firefox prompt you each time or set a default location by clicking the drop-down box and selecting Other.

[2] Change the behaviour of the download manager. If you uncheck Show Download Manager you'll never see it except for a notification when files are done.

[3] When certain files are recognised by Firefox you can change their behaviour by clicking the Change Action button and choosing an alternative program association. This will only affect Firefox and not the rest of Windows.

## Timesaver tip

Anytime you're in the browser, press Ctrl+J to bring up the Firefox Download Manager. Also, if you've chosen a default save location, you can save any file to an alternate directory by right-clicking and choosing Save As.

6

# Configuring
# Firefox (cont.)

## Use advanced options

**1** The Advanced tab contains a selection of miscellaneous settings, including the settings for SSL security and site validation.

**2** Two of the most useful options are tabbed browsing and software update. The tabbed browsing settings will change the way Firefox's tabbed browsing featuring behaves. For example, you can have links from other applications run in the current tab or open a new tab or have Firefox display a warning if you attempt to close the browser with two or more tabs open.

**3** Software update monitors the Firefox server for new program updates. It also alerts you to new versions of any Extensions you have installed.

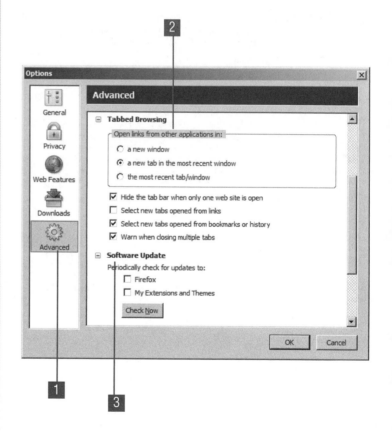

Among Firefox's many features, Extensions are considered to be one of the 'killer apps'. Tiny, free software modules created by Firefox users that extend the browsers capabilities, hundreds of Extensions can be downloaded from the Firefox website and whether you think you need them or not it's almost guaranteed that something will catch your eye. Thanks to the way Firefox has been designed, installing and managing Extensions is dead easy.

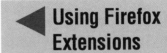

# Using Firefox Extensions

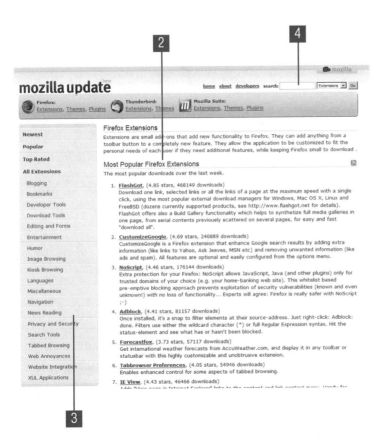

## Download and install Extensions

**1** First off, head to the Extensions site at http://addons.mozilla.org and click the Firefox Extensions link.

**2** The most popular extensions are listed on the main page.

**3** Browse the Extension categories with these links to the left.

**4** Select Extensions from the drop-down search box in the top-right corner and enter a search term.

6

# Using Firefox Extensions (cont.)

**5** Click an Extension and you'll be taken to its download page. Read the information here to check the Extension features and requirements.

**6** Check that the Extension supports your version of Firefox. This Extension works with everything from Firefox 0.8 upwards.

**7** Read the user comments to find out if there are any problems, or just to see what other users thought about the Extension.

**8** Make sure that you've got Software Installs enabled in the Firefox options, then click Install Now to begin the installation.

**9** The Software Installation dialog will pop-up, listing the Extension you've chosen. Click Install Now.

Installation only takes a second in most cases and once it's done the Extension window will appear. Usually you will need to restart Firefox.

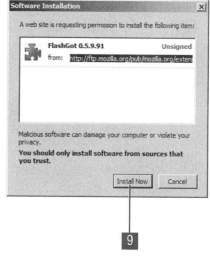

## For your information

One of the most useful Extensions is BugMeNot (www.bugmenot.com), which stores logins for hundreds of sites. The purpose of this is to save you signing up for a free registration every single time you want to view a news article or access any other content. It's a real time-saver and a definite must-have for eager web surfers.

## Use Extensions

1. Most Extensions are used either by right-clicking within Firefox or from a toolbar button. The two Extensions installed in our example, BugMeNot and FlashGot, are both on the right-click menu.

2. For BugMeNot, we simply right-click on a web form and choose the BugMeNot option. Some Extensions will open windows or display further options.

3. From the Firefox toolbar, click Tools and select Extensions. Here you can view and manage your installed Extensions.

4. Click Uninstall to remove the selected Extension.

5. Update will check for newer versions.

6. Options displays settings specific to each Extension.

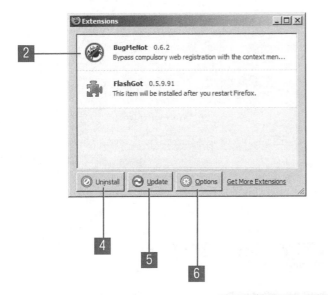

### For your information

To play web content like animation and video you'll need to install Plugins. These are external applications that interface with the browser, taking over for specific functions when needed. To get the most out of the web, you'll need Flash (www.flash.com), Java (http://www.sun.com/java/), Shockwave (www.shockwave.com), Real Player (www.real.com), QuickTime (www.apple.com/quicktime) and the latest version of Media Player (www.microsoft.com).

# Browsing the web with Firefox

Type in the web address and hit Enter – that's pretty much it! Browsing websites is a very painless experience, especially when using Firefox. And despite what the tabloids may say, provided you've got your security suitably beefed up (see Chapter 3) you don't need to worry about viruses, hackers or other unpleasantness. You'll quickly diskover the simple joys of tabbed browsing, too, especially if you've only ever used Internet Explorer before.

## View and navigate websites

1. Type a web address into the address bar and hit enter or click the Go button to visit the site, it will be displayed in the main browser window. Click the arrow on the address bar to see previously visited sites.

2. Firefox includes a built-in search. Type a search term into the box and hit enter.

3. Use the back and forward buttons to move between sites previously viewed in your current session.

4. Click Reload to refresh the current web page.

5. Click the Home button to go back to your defined home page. Set this in the Options menu.

6. The Bookmark toolbar can store your favourite web pages for quick access.

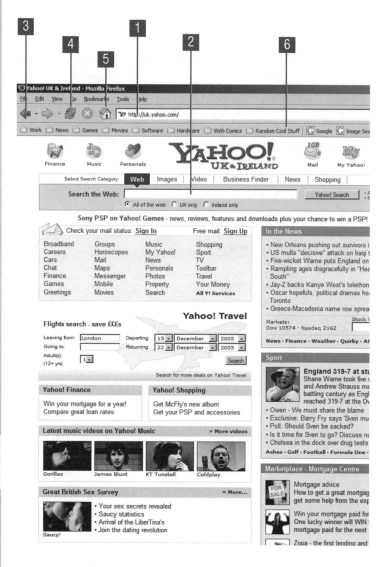

## Timesaver tip

If you type the name of a website into the address bar without putting www. or a domain name, Firefox will run a search and take you to the first matching site. This is useful if you're visiting a popular site like Amazon or IMDB, as you can go there quickly without having to type the full address.

```
Open Link in New Window
Open Link in New Tab

Bookmark This Link...          ────  8
Save Link As...                ──  9
Send Link...
Copy Link Location

⚡ FlashGot Link        Ctrl+F1
🅰 FlashGot All         Ctrl+F3
🌀 Build Gallery
🔗 FlashGot Options              ▶

Properties
```

**7** Right-click on a link or image to bring up further options. The tabbed browsing feature allows you to open links in new tabs as well as new windows, which is very useful for reducing desktop clutter.

**8** Click Bookmark this Link to save the link and add it to your favourites.

**9** Save Link As will allow you to save the linked file to a location on your hard disk. You can also copy the link or send it via email.

## Jargon buster

**HTTP** – HyperText Transfer Protocol, the system used to display web pages, this tells a server that you're visiting to view a website. Sites beginning with www do not have to be prefixed with HTTP but those without, for example images.google.com, must have HTTP placed in front.

**Plugins** – additional software applications that are called by a web browser when needed to perform a specific function. Common plugins include Flash, QuickTime and Shockwave.

## Timesaver tip

Open a new tab quickly in Firefox by hitting Ctrl+T. Open a link in a new tab by holding Ctrl when you click.

6

# Managing bookmarks

If you've not already, you'll soon realise how important and useful the bookmark function is when browsing the web. With the amount of sites out there you need something to help you keep track, and Firefox offers plenty of options for storing your favourite sites. You can bookmark a page just like normal, but also place your very favourite sites in the bookmark toolbar to make them instantly accessible. There's even a user-friendly bookmark manager to help you keep all those links organised.

## Bookmark a site

**1** Want to save a link to that site? Hit Ctrl+D or right-click on the page.

**2** A dialog will appear asking where you want to save the link. Click the drop-down menu and choose Bookmarks, Bookmarks toolbar or one of the recently used folders.

**3** Click Bookmarks from the toolbar and you can view any bookmarks you've saved.

**4** Click Manage Bookmarks to bring up the Bookmarks Manager.

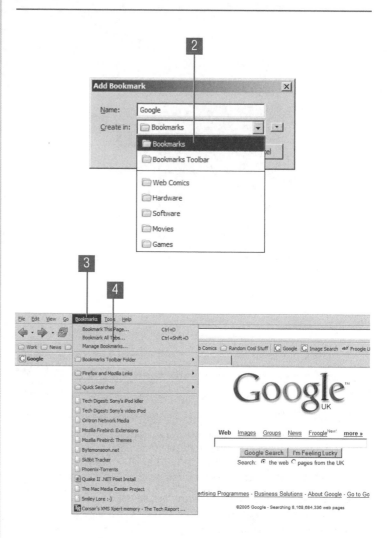

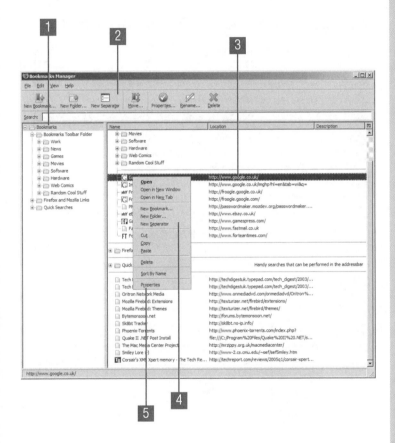

## Edit your bookmarks

**1** Your bookmark folders appear down the side.

**2** Drag links into the Bookmarks Toolbar Folder to add them to your Bookmark toolbar. They will appear in the main Firefox window.

**3** Select a folder and right-click to bring up various options.

**4** You can add a new bookmark, create a new bookmark folder or add a separator to organise your bookmarks.

**5** Click the Properties option from the right-click menu or toolbar to see more info about a folder or link and edit the data.

### Important

If you've got important links stored you should regularly back them up. Click File in the Bookmarks Manager and select Export. You can then save your Bookmarks file to a location on your hard disk. If you need to restore the bookmarks, select the Import option.

6

# Getting an email address

Aside from browsing the web, you'll spend a large amount of your time online sending and receiving email. You'll get a basic email service from your internet service provider but most choose to go with an alternative free or paid-for service offering more features. By far the most popular is Microsoft's Hotmail, but its popularity has meant that good, memorable addresses are increasingly scarce and any account opened gets almost immediately flooded by spam. Thankfully there's no shortage of alternatives. We've chosen Fastmail, a fantastic email provider that provides a basic, but still useful, free service and some reasonably priced premium accounts.

1  Type www.fastmail.co.uk into your web browser and on the front page, click the Sign Up Now link for one of the account types.

2  You'll now need to choose an email address. For free accounts this must be at least seven characters. You can click the drop-down menu to select an alternative domain name.

3  Type a password for your account. Repeat it to confirm you've typed it correctly.

4  Enter your name.

5  You will need to enter another email address so the details of your new account can be confirmed. It's also used to retrieve your account details in case you forget.

6  If another Fastmail user referred you, enter their username here.

7  Read the terms of service and click Agree (if you agree) and then Signup.

8  Read the confirmation mail that is sent to your alternate address and click the link to activate your account.

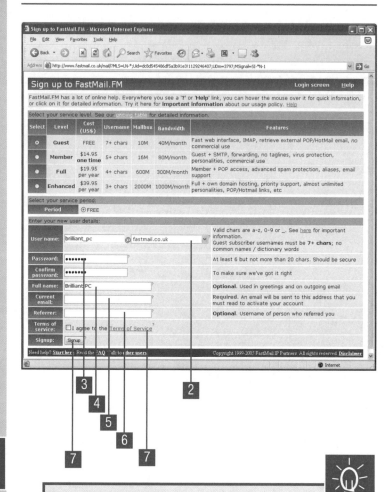

## Important

Fastmail checks the password you enter when signing up – if it sees a dictionary word you'll be asked to confirm that you want to have it, as such words are very easy to crack. For the best security you should use a mix of numbers and letters.

## Jargon buster

**Spam** – junk email, named after the food product or the famous Monty Python sketch, depending on who you ask. Spam has become a huge problem with billions of mails sent every year hawking anything from Viagra to dubious loan offers. Most, if not all, email providers should now have some level of spam filtering.

Compared to the fairly simplistic interface of Hotmail, Fastmail can appear quite confusing at first. This is only because it packs so many features however and once you've got used to the large number of options it's as easy to use as any other webmail service. Of course, once you do understand all the functions available you'll find it a far more flexible service than most other email providers.

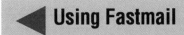

## Using Fastmail

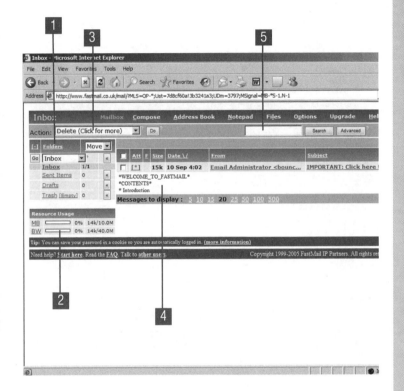

### Use the Fastmail interface

**1** Your inbox and other folders are listed down the left-hand side.

**2** The Resource Usage meters show how much of your storage space and bandwidth have been used. Paid accounts include larger bandwidth limits.

**3** Use the drop-down Action menu, check the box next to the message(s) you want to perform the action on, then click the Do button.

**4** Email is displayed here. Click the From address to send a mail, or the subject to read the message.

**5** Search your messages.

## Timesaver tip

Don't have an alternate email address? There's a site that can help you – www.mailinator.com. You can send mail to anything @ mailinator.com and it creates a temporary inbox. Go to the site, type in the address you used and your mail will be waiting. This is great for avoiding spam when you want to sign up for message boards, or if you need to use a service like Fastmail and you don't already have an address. Remember though, the alternate address in Fastmail is used to retrieve your login details when you've forgotten them and since Mailinator doesn't use any passwords, you should change it as soon as possible.

6

# Sending an email

▶

## Timesaver tip

If you're sending a mass email and don't want everyone to see the other email addresses, put all the recipients in the BCC field and your own address in the To field.

**1** Click Compose.

**2** In the From box, you can select an alternative address to send mail from by clicking the arrow to display other personalities.

**3** Click the Change button to enter a custom From address.

**4** In the To field, type in the address to which you're sending email; separate addresses with a comma to send to multiple recipients.

**5** Use the Cc field to send a copy of the mail to another address.

**6** Bcc will send a copy to the specified addresses without revealing the recipients' details to other people receiving the message.

**7** Click Address Book to add stored names to the To, Cc and Bcc fields.

**8** To attach a file to your message, click Browse and select it from your disks.

**9** When you're done entering the details for your email, click Send. To save it for later, click Save Draft.

Once you've sent an email, you'll be shown a confirmation and asked if you want to add unrecognised addresses to your Address Book.

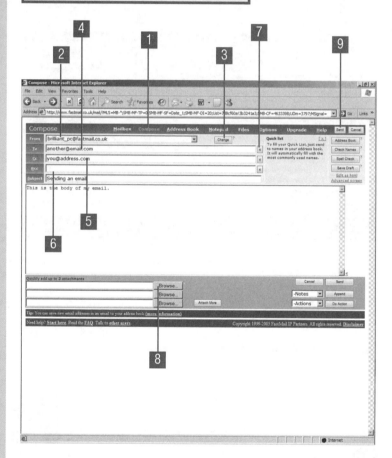

## Important

Be careful when attaching files to your email. Not only does the free Fastmail service have a limited bandwidth allowance for sending and receiving mail, but most servers will reject large attachments. Try not to send anything larger than about 1 MB unless you know the person receiving it can accept the file.

Fastmail has an extensive range of options and features that allow you to customise the behaviour of the interface and the way it handles emails. As well as the standard array of user preferences, you can use an advanced rules system to protect against unwanted messages, by rejecting email based on specified criteria or shuttling it into a particular folder. It is easy to set up auto-respond and forwarding for your messages, but the rule options are deceptively simple. As you become more accustomed to its features it's possible to use complex commands and perform all manner of useful tricks. Although Fastmail's spam protection features work incredibly well, you can use the rules to define your own custom spam filters.

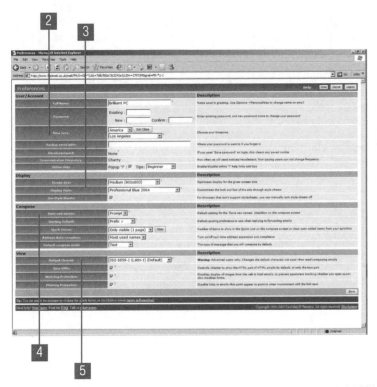

# Configuring Fastmail

## Change your account preferences

1 Click Options, then Preferences.

2 In the User/Account section, you can change the name that appears when you send email, change the backup email address and set your time zone.

3 In Display, you can match the Fastmail interface to your screen resolution and select an alternative style sheet.

4 Use the Compose options to change settings for sending email, such as auto-completing addresses and text entry mode.

5 Don't change the View settings unless you're sure about what you're doing. Not only do these options affect the character set for typing and reading mails, there are also some important settings that protect you from phishing and spam mails.

## Jargon buster

**Phishing** – a con using fake email and websites that tricks victims into entering sensitive details for online banks and other services such as Paypal and Ebay. The emails often tell you that your account is going to expire and give a link to reactivate. Although the link looks genuine it is actually going to a totally different location set-up by the scammers. Phishing mails can often be spotted by the abundance of spelling and grammar mistakes, but in any case banks and other sites will not ever ask you to enter your details via email.

6

# Configuring Fastmail (cont.)

## Create custom rules

**1** From the Options screen, click Define Rules.

**2** You can automatically reject emails that meet certain criteria. First select where Fastmail should check, by selecting from the 'Look In' category drop-down menu.

**3** Enter the text you want it to search for in Text Matching.

**4** Check the Silent box to reject emails without notifying the sender. Click Add to save the new rule.

**5** Manage messages with large attachments by entering a maximum file size and choosing whether you want to reject them straight off or move to another folder.

**6** Enter a secret word and give it to your friends. They can use that in the subject line and their messages will always bypass the filters you set up.

## Timesaver tip

Block email from an entire domain by selecting the From option and just entering '@TheDomainYouWantToBlock.com' into the text matching field. This will reject all messages coming from any address at this domain and is useful for blocking persistent spammers. Don't do it unless you're sure you're not going to need email from there!

**7** Automatically move messages matching criteria you choose into a specific folder using the Mailing Lists/ File Into Folders filter.

**8** As before, tell Fastmail where to look and enter some text for the filter, but you'll also need to choose which folder you want the messages moved into.

**9** You can set an away auto-response by checking the Enable Vacation Message box and typing your message into the text box. This message will be automatically sent to anyone who emails you when it's active.

# Making the most of Fastmail's features

Among the many features Fastmail offers, two in particular stand out. Its Personalities function allows you to create new personalities for sending email, so you can make it look as though email is coming from another location and use an alternative address for receiving replies, helping to keep your messages organised. The other is the POP Links feature. Enter the login details for a POP3 or Hotmail account and Fastmail will check those accounts for new mail, delivering them to your Inbox (or any other folder.) Combined with the Personalities option, this allows you to manage separate email accounts under one interface.

## Create new Personalities

**1** Go to Options and click the Personalities link.

**2** Double-click on Create New to start entering the details for the personality.

**3** Enter a display name – this will be what people receiving messages see.

**4** Enter your full name.

**5** Choose a From address. This can be anything, but when people reply they'll be replying to that address, so if it's fake you won't get any responses.

**6** Optionally, you can enter your mobile number. Fastmail includes a text messaging feature which requires your mobile number to work.

**7** Select a signature. You can use the default or create one in the Signatures section of the Options menu.

**8** Select the folder where copies of messages you've sent will be stored.

**9** Click Save to store the personality and Done to exit the section. It will now be available in the From menu when you compose a new message.

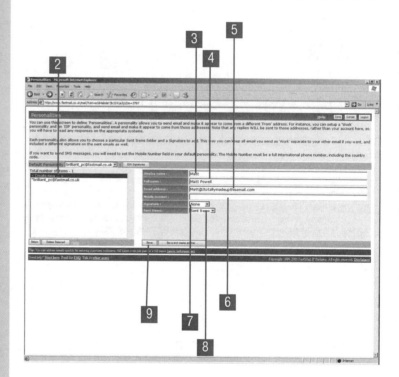

## Timesaver tip

Personalities can be incredibly useful if you occasionally work from home or want to separate professional email from personal. Just set up a Personality with your work email as the From address, and when you message from home it'll look like you're slogging away in the office. Don't forget that replies will be sent to whatever email address you give.

## Retrieve Hotmail and ISP email through Fastmail

1. Go to Pop Links in the Options menu and start creating a new POP link.

2. Choose a display name for your POP mailbox. Make it memorable.

3. Select whether you want to retrieve mail from a POP or Hotmail account.

4. Enter the server and server port details. If you do not know these, contact your email provider. Leave blank if you chose Hotmail.

5. Type in the username and password you use to login to the account.

6. Choose the folder in which you want the retrieved messages to be placed.

7. Select how long messages will be kept on the original server. This can be up to 6 months and would allow you to download them again if you lose the copies.

8. Choose whether to check for new mail manually or automatically, every few hours.

9. If Disabled is checked, it means Fastmail has failed to connect to the server five times in a row. Check that the details are correct then clear Disabled and save.

10. If you wish to download messages again, use the Clear Stored IDs option. If the originals are still on the POP server they will be retrieved the next time the account is checked.

6

# Configuring MSN Messenger

Instant Messaging is a great way of keeping in contact with friends and relatives across the world. Once you have your friends on your contact list, you'll be able to see whenever they're online and chat to them in real-time. You can also send files and even use voice and video chat. There are many different Instant Messaging applications available, such as AOL Instant Messenger, ICQ, Skype and Yahoo! Messenger, but for this example we'll be using Microsoft's MSN Messenger since it's the most popular Instant Messenger network and can be used instantly by anyone who has a Hotmail or Passport account.

## Download Messenger

1. Visit http://messenger.msn.com

2. If you already have a Hotmail or Passport account, just click the Registered MSN User link to start downloading Messenger.

3. If you have not registered previously, you'll need to click the link for either creating a Hotmail account or signing up using another email address.

4. Once the sign-up is completed, you'll be directed to download MSN Messenger.

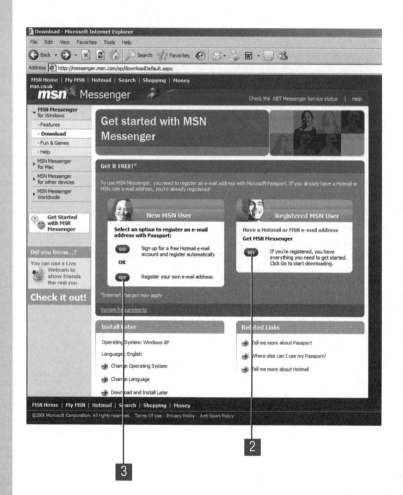

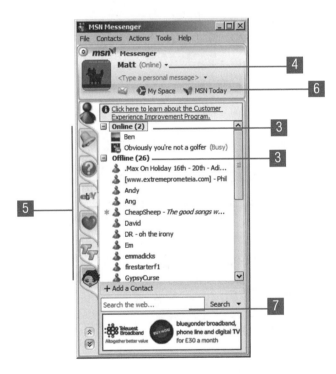

## Use the MSN Interface

1 When Messenger is installed, its icon will be displayed in your system tray. Double-click this to bring up the login screen, enter the email address and password you chose for your account.

2 Tick the Sign in Automatically box and Messenger will remember your login details and sign you in each time you boot into Windows.

3 Your contacts are listed in the main window, change the way they're organised by using the Sort Contacts By option in the Contacts menu.

4 Your details are shown at the top, with your name and picture.

5 These tabs allow you to switch between different services available through Messenger. For example, you can browse Ebay or receive help using Messenger.

6 Click MSN Today to see the latest news relating to MSN and Messenger.

7 Search the web via MSN Search by entering a term in the search field.

## Important

If you're on a shared system do not allow Messenger to store your details and sign-in automatically, otherwise anyone using that PC will have access to your account.

# Managing Contacts

Messenger is useless without having your friends on it to chat, so the first thing you'll want to do is to add them to your contact list. You do this by inputting their email address – if they have not registered with MSN you can send them an email asking them to get online so you can chat. If they have registered, contacts will be asked if they want you to add them first, you will also see the same prompt when someone attempts to add you to their contact list. You may also want to delete contacts from your list, or you can block them so it looks as though you're always offline.

## Add a contact

**1** On the main interface, either click Add a Contact or go to the Contacts menu and select Add a Contact.

**2** Choose whether you want to add a contact by their email address or phone number.

**3** Enter the details and click Next to begin adding them.

**4** If the contact is signed up with MSN, you'll get a 'success' message and they'll see a prompt asking if they want to be added.

**5** If they are not yet signed up with MSN and you want to send them a reminder to register, you can type a greeting into the text box.

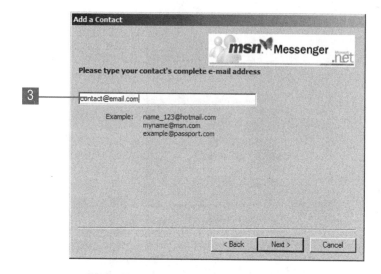

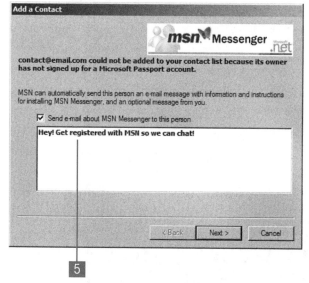

## Delete and block contacts

**1** Right-click on a contact, online or off, to see a list of options.

**2** Send them an email or message. Offline contacts cannot be sent messages.

**3** Block the contact from seeing you online.

**4** View their profile, which could includes details like age, sex and location, depending on what they've entered.

**5** If you've created a contact group, group options allow you to move the contact into there.

**6** Delete a contact to remove them from your contact list – you will no longer be able to message them. When you do this you will be given the option to block them as well.

---

**MSN Messenger**

File   Contacts   Actions   Tools   Help

**msn** Messenger

**Matt** (Online) ▾

<Type a personal message> ▾

My Space   MSN Today

ℹ Click here to learn about the Customer Experience Improvement Program.

⊟ Online (1)
   ■ Ben
⊟ Offline (27)

Send E-mail — **2**
Send Other ▸

Audio/Video ▸
Start an Activity
Play a Game

View Message History

Block — **3**
View This Person's Contact Card
View Profile — **4**
Group Options ▸ — **5**
Delete Contact — **6**

Add a Mobile Number for This Contact

Search the web...

6

# Communicating with Messenger

The main purpose of MSN Messenger is, of course, communication. You can open a chat window with any of your online contacts and begin talking to them instantly. You can also send and receive files and play games. Messenger includes a wide range of plugins and extra add-ons you can download to add new animations and features, so you can irritate your friends with smileys and animations or draw silly pictures with the whiteboard function.

## Chat with your contacts

**1** Double-click on an online contact to bring up a chat window.

**2** Type your messages into the text input box and hit Enter or press Send.

**3** The conversation will appear in the main window.

**4** Use the icons above the text input to add smileys and other animated icons and emoticons, or change your text font and color.

**5** Click the whiteboard tab to draw pictures. Provided the other person is using a compatible version of Messenger with whiteboard installed, you can draw and send doodles.

**6** Your picture and your contacts picture are shown at the side. Click the lower arrow to change your picture and the side arrow to hide the pictures.

**7** You can invite other contacts into the chat by clicking Invite then selecting an online contact.

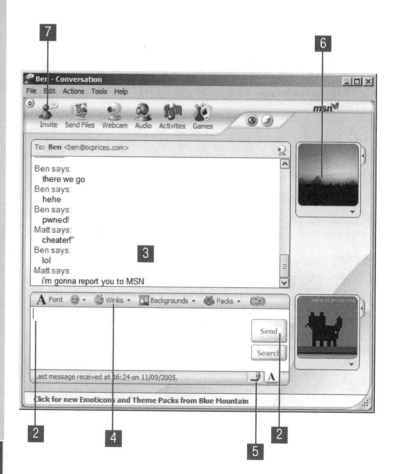

## Jargon buster

**Emoticons** – emotional icons are used in chat to show a particular feeling, like the emoticon for happy :) and sad :( . Often referred to as smileys.

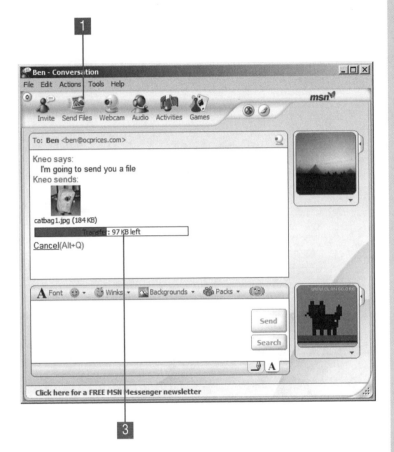

---

### Send files

**1** Send a file by either right-clicking in the contact list, choosing Send Other and then Send a File or Photo or clicking Send Files from the toolbar of an active chat window.

**2** Select the file you want to send when prompted, then wait for the other person to accept.

**3** You'll be shown the file progress in the chat window. Click Cancel to end it.

### Important

Be careful about accepting executable files, word documents and other files that could transmit viruses. If the file is coming from someone you don't know and you didn't ask for it, you should check it with your virus scanner. If your virus scanner has an option for watching Instant Messaging enable this as it will help protect against worms that use Instant Messaging to spread.

6

# Sending and receiving files (cont.)

## Receive files

**1** When receiving a file, you will need to accept it before the transfer will begin.

**2** If you click Save As rather than accept, you can save to another location on your hard disk.

**3** Click Decline to reject the file.

**4** When the file is completed, you can click the link to open it.

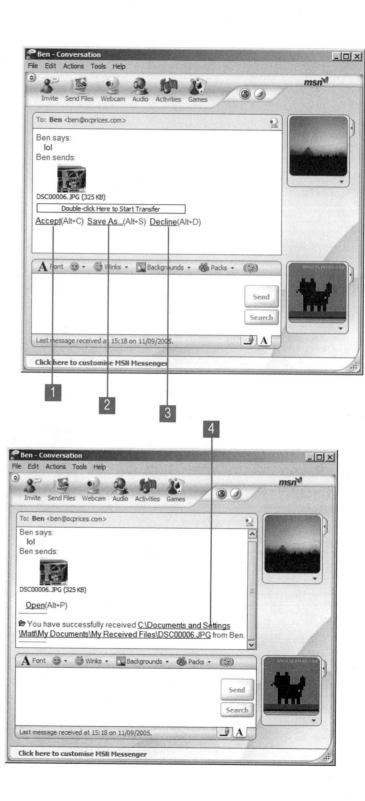

# Multimedia

## Introduction

The main attraction of a PC is their versatility, whether it's browsing the web, working, or playing games. This has really come into play in the last few years as the popularity of digital media has increased rapidly, helped along by the internet, ever-faster broadband connections, digital cameras and DVD video. In this chapter we're going to look at three key areas – images, music and video – and how you can use your PC to view, manage and use your media. Digital cameras are standard issue now, chances are you've got a rapidly growing collection of images stored on your hard disk, so we'll look at how you view those pictures and also create a slideshow for friends and family (and backing up your precious snaps in the process.) Anyone who has shelves bulging with audio CDs should read up on how to digitise albums, allowing you to use them in MP3 players, mobile phones and other devices, as well as creating your own compilations to save wear and tear on the originals. And if you've got a DVD burner and lots of digital videos on your hard disk, the final section of this chapter will tell you about playing video files and DVDs on your computer as well as helping you create your very own DVD disk that can be played back on most standalone players.

## What you'll do

**View images**

**Create a photo slideshow**

**Listen to music**

**Tune into Internet radio**

**Rip audio CDs**

**Create your own audio CD**

**Play videos and DVDs**

**Create a DVD**

# Viewing images

If you want to view standard JPG and GIF images within Windows, you can (thankfully) do it without any additional software. The basic Picture and Fax Viewer that's included with every version does a perfectly adequate job of browsing images and you can configure folders to preview all the pictures they contain. It may not handle the more obscure image formats but then there are plenty of alternative photo editing and viewing applications to be found online, assuming you haven't got one already bundled with your PC or digital camera.

## View images within folders

**1** Locate the folder containing your images, right-click and choose properties.

**2** Click the Customize tab.

**3** From the drop-down menu, select Photo Album or Pictures.

**4** You can assign an image to the folder to remind you of its contents, click Choose Picture to do this.

**5** Click Change Icon to select an alternative folder icon.

**6** Click Apply.

**7** Open the folder.

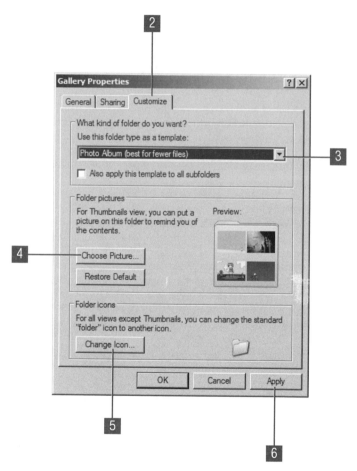

### Jargon buster

**GIF** – Graphics Interchange Format, pronounced 'giff', commonly used on the web for images because it can be compressed, but not often for photos as it has limited color depth compared to JPG.

**JPG** – popular image format, its full name is JPEG or Joint Photographic Expert Group. Often used for photos.

**8** In the folder, click the Views menu.

**9** You'll have a new Filmstrip option, click this to display all the images in a row along the bottom of the folder window.

**10** Click an image once to display it in the folder, or twice to open it in the associated application.

**11** Use the arrows to move from one image to the next.

**12** See a slideshow of all the images in the folder by clicking View as Slideshow in the Picture Tasks menu.

## For your information

Your digital camera images can be transferred to your PC in two ways. First is by using the supplied software and USB cable. Any camera should include even basic applications for transferring, editing and viewing images. Usually some form of simple Photo Editor and a manager/viewer combination that grabs your pictures when you plug in your digicam. The second option is to use a card reader, since the pictures are generally stored on a removable memory card. Get yourself an inexpensive USB reader (most handle five, six or seven types of memory card) and you can transfer your pics to any system just by dragging and dropping them off the card.

# Viewing images (cont.)

## View images with Picture and Fax Viewer

**1** Access Picture and Fax Viewer by either double-clicking on an image or right-clicking, select Open With and then Picture and Fax Viewer.

**2** Use the left and right arrows to move back and forth between the images. You can also use the keyboard cursor keys.

**3** Press the Actual Size button to view the full size of the image. When you do this, the Best Fit button to the left will become active and is used to switch back to the previous view.

**4** Zoom in and out.

**5** You can rotate images using these buttons but it automatically saves over the original picture. Make sure you've got a backup copy before doing this.

## Timesaver tip

There are specialised applications specifically for viewing images, the most popular of which is ACDSee (www.acdsee.com). Not only does ACDSee offer an easy way to view your images but it also acts as a photo editor and management tool, so you can keep track of all your pictures.

So you've got hundreds of photos taken with a digital camera on your PC. What now? You can print them out, but good quality paper and printer ink is expensive. One of the best ways to show off your holiday snaps is to create a slideshow on CD or DVD that friends and relations can play through their TV or computer. For this, we'll be using CyberLink's PowerProducer, a simple multimedia tool that is often found bundled with digital cameras, printers, PC systems and DVD drives. You can download a trial from www.gocyberlink.com but you may have a full version already.

## Select a disk type and images

1  From the main menu, choose Produce Movie disk.

2  You'll next need to choose your disk format and size. Click Next to continue.

3  In the next step, click the Photos button from the content menu.

4  A browse window will open automatically. Locate the folder containing your images and select any you want to include.

5  Click Open.

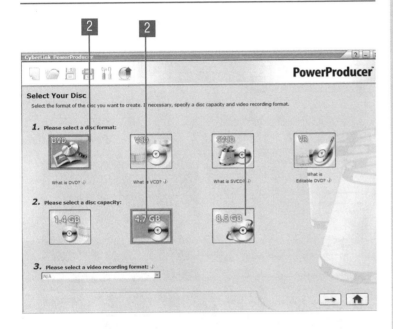

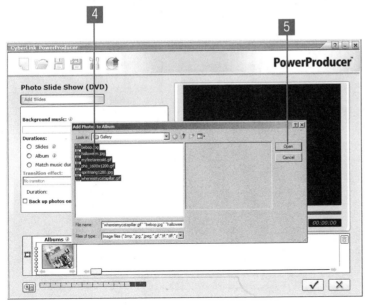

# Creating a DVD slideshow (cont.)

## Edit your slideshow

**1** Your images will now be loaded into the slideshow. You can drag and drop to change their position.

**2** Right-click on the album in the filmstrip to view its properties and change its name.

**3** Change the display duration of each slide and the entire album. If you leave the album duration blank the slideshow will loop indefinitely.

**4** Select a transition effect from the drop-down menu to add a bit of glitz to your slideshow.

**5** Check the Back Up Photos option if you want the original pictures to be saved on the disk as well.

**6** Use these playback controls to view a preview of your slideshow.

**7** Click to set the currently selected image as the cover image for the album.

**8** Watch this meter to ensure that you don't exceed the maximum capacity for your disk.

**9** View information about the album, such as file size.

**10** Click to add background audio to your slideshow.

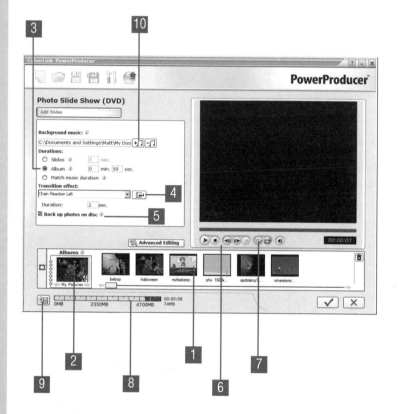

**Background Music**

**Background music:**

C:\Documents and Settings\Matt\My Documents\My

☑ Fade in          ☐ Auto repeat

☑ Fade out

**Trim audio:**

| | |
|---|---|
| Begin: | 00:00:57 |
| End: | 00:04:45 |
| Duration: | 00:03:48 |

**Volume:**

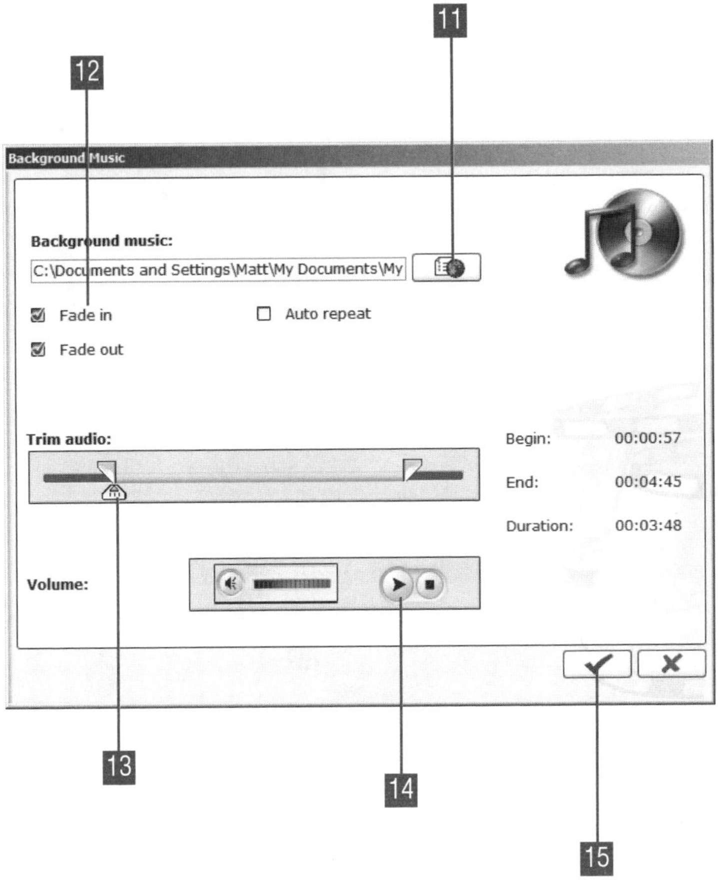

**11** Click Browse and locate the audio track you want to use as background music.

**12** Click the boxes to have a fade in, fade out and auto-repeat the track.

**13** Use the sliders and drag them up and down to trim the beginning and end of the track.

**14** Preview the audio with the playback controls.

**15** Click to confirm and save the changes.

# Creating a DVD slideshow (cont.)

## Edit the main menu

**1** Back in the menu preview, click the Menu button from the Edit section.

**2** Use this screen to customise your main menu. Click the menu text in the preview window and change it to anything you like.

**3** Click to select a different font, color and text size.

**4** You can select an alternative Template by clicking this button and selecting one from the gallery.

**5** It's also possible to change the button layout. In the trial version the amount of changes you can make to the menu and the templates available are limited.

**6** Select a background soundtrack to play for the menu.

**7** The first-play video will show up before the menu each time the disk is loaded. Using this you can insert your own notices and copyright warnings, serious or otherwise.

**8** Save the changes and exit the menu editor.

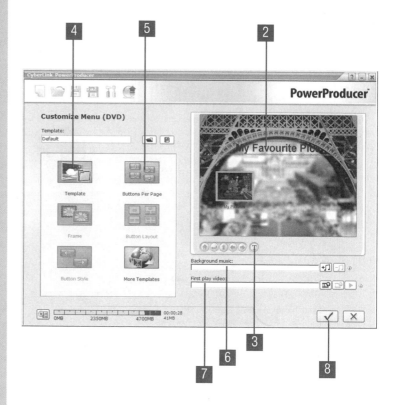

## Important

With options like background music and video it's tempting to add it all to your disk. Don't go overboard though – you'll get fed up of hearing that song loop for the fifth time on a lengthy slideshow. If you're going to put background music on your slideshow go for something subtle and appropriate, and use multiple albums with different audio tracks on each.

## Add to the disk

**1** To add more albums to your disk, click an option from the Import menu. You can then repeat the album creation process and include multiple chapters.

**2** Click an Edit option to edit a particular aspect of your disk.

**3** Preview your disk with the playback controls. Click on a chapter then click Play.

**4** Click the Next button to finish or back to go back a step.

**PowerProducer**

Content (DVD)

**Import**
Video Files
Photos
Scene on DVD

**Capture**
Video

**Edit**
Video clips
Photo Slide Show
Menu
Chapters

Author    Preview

My Favourite Pic...

My Pictures

Disc Structure

Page: 1/1

0MB    2350MB    4700MB    74MB    00:00:58

# Creating a DVD slideshow (cont.)

## Burn the disk

**1** Make sure the correct drive is selected. Click Configure to choose an alternative optical drive.

**2** If the disk is a re-writable CD or DVD, click the Erase Disk Content to clear it.

**3** Enter a name for your disk. This can be anything up to sixteen characters in length.

**4** Check Burn to Disk to burn your slideshow straight to a CD or DVD. You can also set how many copies you want to create.

**5** If you select the Disk Image option, your slideshow will be saved as an image to the hard drive.

**6** Create a DVD folder to save your slideshow as raw DVD files. These can then be burnt to disk using any standard disk burning tool, such as Nero Burning ROM or Easy CD.

**7** Click the Browse buttons to select a location on your hard disk for the disk image and DVD folder, when applicable.

**8** Click to finalise the settings and commit your slideshow to a disk.

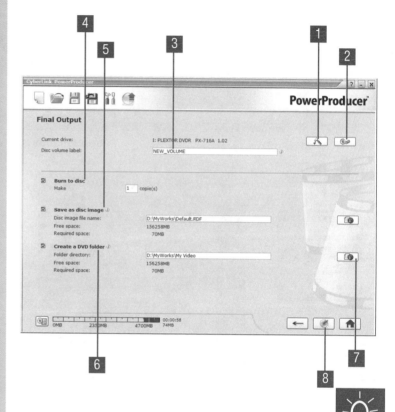

## Jargon buster

**Disk image** – a single file that contains the entire contents of a CD or DVD. You can burn copies safe in the knowledge that each duplicate will be identical.

**ID3 tag** – part of every MP3 is given over to holding data about the track, like title, artist, year and genre. This is the ID3 tag. It's used by MP3 players, hardware and software, to display information about a file.

**Kbps** – Kilobits per second, used in reference to audio files to measure the quality of a track. 128kbps is considered CD quality but music fans claim they can hear the difference and prefer songs to be encoded as high as possible. As you increase the kbps the file size also gets larger.

**MP3** – MPEG audio layer 3, the most popular digital audio format thanks to its ability to compress audio tracks to a fraction of their size without losing too much of the quality.

Windows XP comes ready to playback the most common types of audio files. You can use Windows Media Player, but it's a rather bloated and awkward bit of software, so of course we're going to be using an alternative. Winamp is a powerful, feature-packed and slick jukebox that's considered to be the best media player tool for the PC. It can be downloaded for free from www.winamp.com. You can also upgrade to a Pro version which gives you some extra features, most notably the option to convert audio CDs to MP3. Winamp also makes it easy to edit the ID3 tag information of MP3s and organise your music collection with its Media Library.

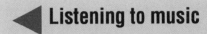

## Play music with Winamp

**1** Double-click on an MP3 or any other audio file and, assuming it's associated, it will open in Winamp. You can use 'Open With' to open with Winamp otherwise.

**2** The top window shows information about the song playing, including information on Kbps and KHz.

**3** Drag this slider to change the position of the track.

**4** Bring up the visualizer/video window. Visualizer displays an animation that moves in time to your music.

**5** Audio playback controls.

**6** Change the volume with this slider.

**7** Click PL to view and hide the playlist window. ML opens up Media Library, which can be used to catalogue your songs.

**8** This is your playlist. Songs that are currently playing or queued will be listed. You can add songs to the playlist by dragging and dropping from anywhere on your PC. Change their position in the playlist by dragging tracks to where you want them.

**9** Click Manage Playlist to Save, Clear or open a new playlist. Change the size of the window by dragging the corner.

**Multimedia 195**

# Listening to
# music (cont.)

## Edit track information

**1** Right-click on a file in your playlist and choose View File Info.

**2** Enter the relevant information into the fields for either ID3v1 or v2. It's best to do both so your songs will display best in devices that support one or the other.

**3** Save time by using the Copy To and Copy From buttons to transfer information from one field to another.

**4** Click Update to save the information.

### For your information

Audio CDs are associated to a program like a normal audio file. When you insert an audio disk Windows will ask whether you want to open it and what program you wish to use. Media Player is associated with CDs by default but Winamp can take over when it's installed.

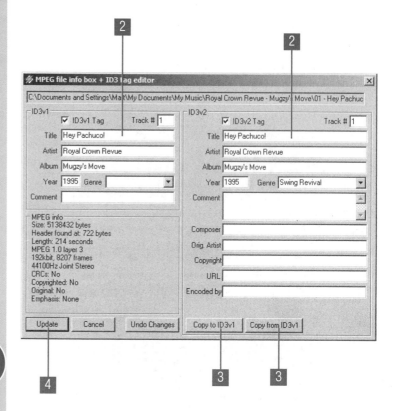

Internet radio has grown to be a huge phenomenon and, in a situation not dissimilar to the infamous pirate radio of the 1980s, has developed from an amateur hobby to full commercial venture. In the early days, stations were operated by individuals using standard PC equipment, broadcasting to a small number of users in a forum or chat room. But as the popularity of streaming audio grew, traditional stations entered the fray, using the web to distribute their shows globally, or specialised companies have sprung up offering home users a hassle-free method of becoming DJs. The most well-known of these is Live365.com, a service that offers an enormous range of stations covering every conceivable taste at a very reasonable price. You can pay for full membership, but the standard free membership lets you listen for nothing, if you don't mind a slightly lower quality and the occasional advert.

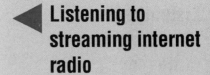

### Search Live365

1 Open your web browser and go to www.live365.com.

2 Type the genre of music or type of broadcast you're after into the search field.

3 You can also browse genres by selecting one from the list.

4 Once you've signed up for an account, enter your login details here. Everyone must be a basic free member to at least listen to stations, but you don't have to join if you're just browsing.

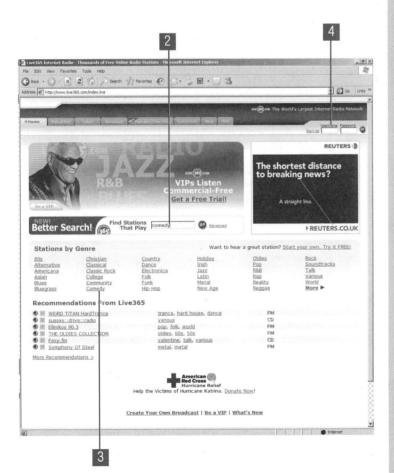

# Listening to streaming internet radio (cont.)

**5** When you search you'll see a list of all the stations that match the criteria.

**6** Click the speaker icons to open the player window. The gold VIP icons indicate a station that is full and available to paying members only.

## For your information

Shoutcast is a technology developed by Nullsoft, the people behind Winamp, that allows anyone to become a DJ. You can use the free software to broadcast from home or listen to thousands of amateur stations worldwide using Winamp. Click over to www.shoutcast.com to find out more.

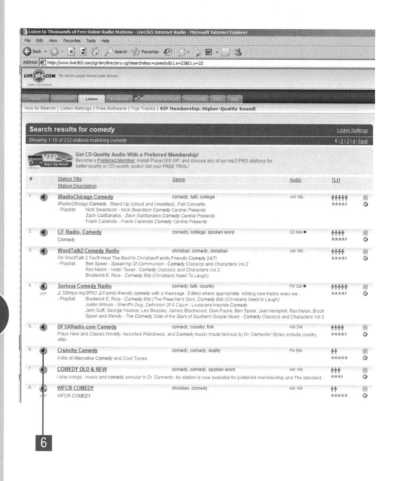

## Use the Live365 Player

**1** The track currently playing is highlighted, and the player will also show you the previous track.

**2** Click to add the track to your wish list. You can view further information on saved tracks by clicking the wish list button.

**3** Rate the track. This helps the station operator know what's popular.

**4** Standard Play and Stop buttons for controlling the playback.

**5** Control the volume.

**6** Add the station to your favourites so you can access it quicker in the future.

### For your information

At the time of writing, the Firefox web browser isn't compatible with Live365. However, when the player window opens you'll be asked if you want to open or download a .PLS file. This is a standard playlist file and if you open this in Winamp you can listen to the radio broadcast. This actually works out better, because if you save it to your hard disk you can listen whenever you want without having to go through the website, just by opening the file.

# Setting-up Winamp for CD-ripping ▶

If you've got a portable audio player or want to listen to your music collection without constantly swapping disks, converting your albums to digital audio files is the only way to go. Using any of the countless CD 'ripping' applications you can extract the audio from a compact disk and convert it to the digital format, which can then be played back on every popular portable audio player or computer system. Once your collection is converted not only is it easy to catalogue and manage your songs, but you save wear and tear on the precious originals stored safely in their jewel cases. We'll be using Winamp to accomplish this. Although you must register the program to create MP3 audio tracks, you can rip to WMA and AAC using the 'Full' free version of Winamp. Although it lacks the advanced options found in a specialised application, Winamp is incredibly easy to use.

## Set encoder options

1. Open Winamp, go to Options, Preferences and then CD Ripping.

2. Choose an encoder. We're going to use WMA since it's widely supported.

3. Set the Encoder Format to Windows Media Audio 9.1.

4. Select a Profile from the drop-down menu. If you know what you're doing you can set the individual settings manually. We'd recommend using the 320Kbps, 44khz Stereo CBR option.

5. Save your settings.

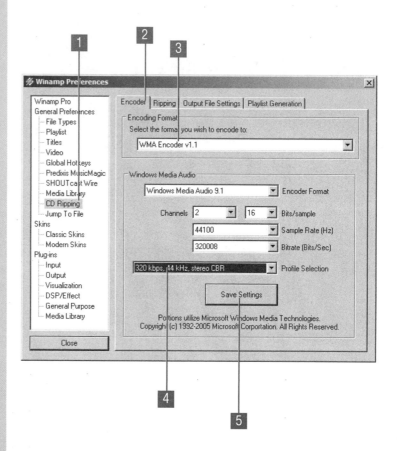

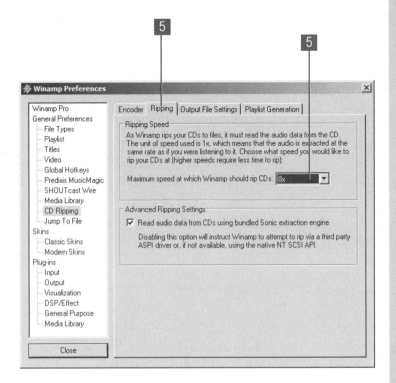

**5** In the Ripping tab you can set the read speed. This is limited to 8x in the free version.

## Jargon buster

**AAC** – Advanced Audio Coding, an audio format that is used most notably by Apple for its iPod audio players.

**WMA** – Windows Media Audio. Competing digital audio format developed by Microsoft. WMA can include DRM so is a popular format for online stores selling music downloads. Most players support WMA (though some can't read its DRM) but one notable exception is Apple's iPod range.

# Setting-up Winamp for CD-ripping (cont.)

## Select output settings

1. Click Output File Settings.

2. Select a folder for your ripped files by clicking Browse.

3. Specify how you want tracks to be named. Click Format Help to see more information.

4. Select whether ripped files should be added to the Winamp Media Library.

5. This option will add data about the track to the ID3 tag.

6. Type in a comment to be added to the comments field of all your songs.

7. Click Playlist Generation.

8. Choose what playlist files you wish to create for your ripped songs.

9. Choose a name for your playlists in the same way as you did for the tracks themselves.

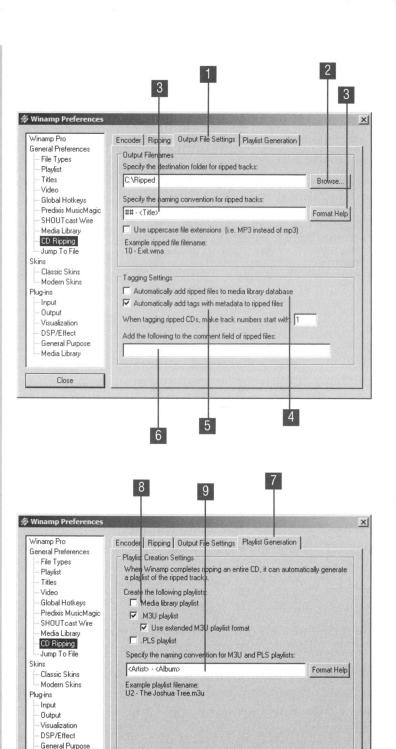

Once you've configured Winamp you can start to rip the audio tracks. This is done simply through Winamp's Media Library interface. The time it takes to rip will vary depending on the speed you've configured through Winamp, the number of tracks you're ripping and the speed of your optical drive. Once it's done, you'll have a complete digital copy of your album waiting on the hard disk.

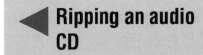

## Rip a CD with Winamp

**1** Bring up Media Library by clicking the ML button on Winamp's main interface.

**2** In the sidebar, choose the optical drive containing your audio CD from the devices list.

**3** If it hasn't already, Winamp will connect to the CDDB and download information about the album.

**4** Click the rip button and select Rip Selected Tracks or Rip All Tracks.

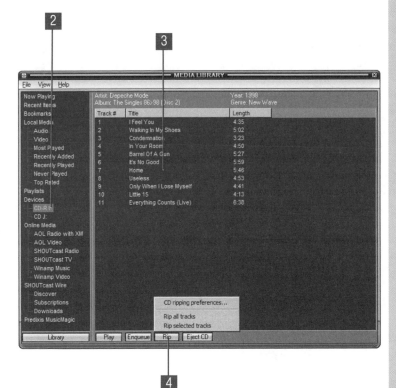

# Ripping an audio CD (cont.)

**5** Information about the rip is displayed at the top of the screen, including the estimated file size.

**6** The Status column shows which tracks are completed, queued or in progress.

**7** Click Rip Options to change preferences for the current rip. Setting the priority will tell the system how important it is and therefore how much of its resources it should dedicate to the task.

**8** If necessary, you can cancel the rip.

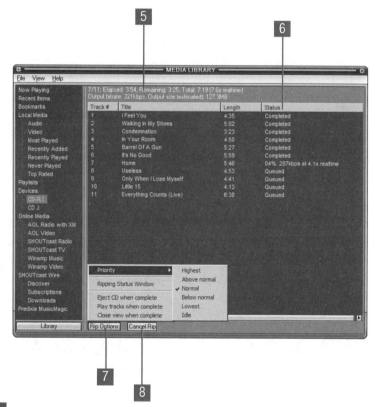

## Jargon buster

**CDDB** – Compact Disk Database. Many audio players, such as Winamp, use the online Gracenote CDDB to automatically gather song information. There is also a free competitor, the freedb (www.freedb.org)

## Important

Disk drives can be extremely sensitive about dust and marks on a CD. If your drive has problems reading a track you'll notice popping, hisses and even gaps in the song when it's played back. Make sure the disk is clean before ripping to ensure you get the best quality possible.

Once you've got your albums digitised, you can download them to an MP3 player or listen to them through your PC. In addition, it's possible to create your own audio CDs, which is really useful if you want to make a compilation of favourite tracks or have a backup of an album that you can safely leave in the car. This is incredibly easy to accomplish since every major CD/DVD burning application around now includes the ability to make a CD from digital audio files. We're going to do this using Nero Burning ROM, one of the most popular disk creation tools around.

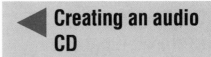

## Creating an audio CD

7

## Select disk options

1 Start Nero, and from the new compilation wizard choose the CD option from the drop-down menu.

2 Select Audio CD.

3 You can enter CD Text info in these fields. This can be read by some CD players.

4 Click the Burn tab.

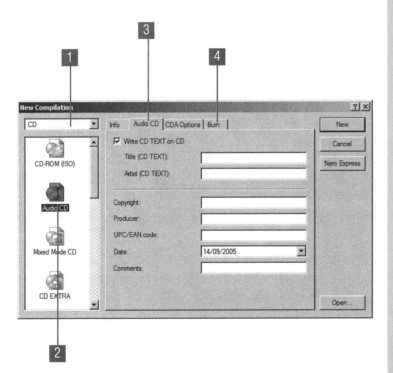

# Creating an
# audio CD (cont.)

5　Use Simulation to check that the disk will burn correctly.

6　If using Simulation, you can disable Write so that the disk will not be written when the simulation is successful. Otherwise, leave it enabled.

7　Check Finalize if it is not selected.

8　Choose a write speed. If you have problems burning try using a lower setting. Leave the write method on the default selection.

9　Enter the number of copies you wish to make.

10　If BURN-Proof is available and not selected, check this box.

11　When you're finished selecting the options for the disk, click New.

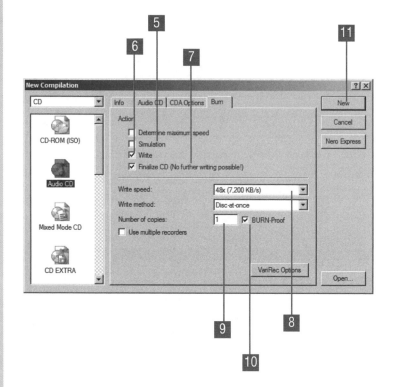

### Add your tracks

**1** Locate the folder containing your music.

**2** Select the songs you want to add to your new CD and drag them into the disk window on the left.

**3** Watch the bar at the bottom of the screen. This tells you how much of the disk you've taken up. If it goes yellow, it means you're dangerously close to full capacity and it may not be able to fit everything onto the disk. If it turns red, that means you've gone past maximum capacity.

**4** Select songs in the disk window and press Delete to remove them from the compilation. This will not remove them from your hard disk.

**5** If you have more than one CD/DVD burner, check that the correct burner is selected.

**6** Click to finish and burn the disk. The disk that's created is a standard audio CD and can be used in the majority of CD and DVD players.

## Important

If the burn is successful but the disk doesn't work, there can be several reasons. First of all you might be using cheap media. Brand-name blank CDs are of a far higher quality and have better compatibility – poor media is also a common cause of burns failing to complete. It could also be the drive, though, as not every CD player can read CD-R disks, so try it in a few other players before binning the disk.

# Playing video files ▶

Windows comes equipped with Media Player, so it can handle the common formats out of the box. It's not quite that simple, of course, since there are many different types of video files available. If you download a video file from the internet, there's a good chance it won't work until you installed the correct decoder software. In any case, you may want to choose an alternative video player over Media Player, because its bloated interface can be rather confusing. We've used the excellent VLC media player, a free open-source application which can be downloaded from www.videolan.org, but you may also want to check out BSplayer (www.bsplayer.org). For DVD movies, CyberLink's PowerDVD is the most common application. It has all the features you'd need, is very simple to use and is often bundled with PC systems, DVD burners and graphics cards.

1   Double-click on a video file or choose Open With and select the application you wish to use to view the video. For this example, we're using VLC media player.

2   Standard playback controls for play, pause and stop. Click the eject icon to open a file.

3   Use the buttons on the far left and far right of these four to go back and forward in a playlist. The two in the middle control the playback speed.

4   Change the volume.

5   The viewer window, where your video is display. Double click this to expand the video to full screen.

6   Jump back and forward in a video using this slider.

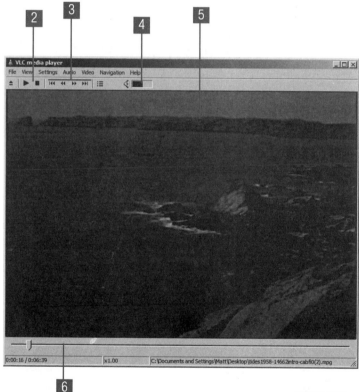

## Timesaver tip

Find out what codecs a file is using by downloading G-Spot from www.headbands.com/gspot. Don't mind the slightly rude name, G-Spot is a great little tool that examines video files and tells you exactly what codec they're using, so you can check files you've downloaded and then search online for the correct codec if it's needed.

```
Play
Next
Previous
Stop

Video Track        ▶        8
Audio Track        ▶        9

Fullscreen
Zoom               ▶
Deinterlace        ▶
Always on top
Wallpaper
Snapshot

Audio Device       ▶
Audio Channels     ▶
Visualisations     ▶
Equaliser          ▶

Switch interface   ▶
Add Interface      ▶
Miscellaneous      ▶
Open               ▶
```

**7** Right-click on the viewer window to bring up a list of options.

**8** Use video track to switch video streams, when applicable. If the video has subtitles, they will appear as an additional option.

**9** The audio track option allows you to select an alternative audio track

## Jargon buster

**Codec** – COmpressor DECompressor. A codec, such as MP3 or Divx, not only provides the capability to decompress (or decode) files for viewing, but also compress (encode) for creating audio and video.

**Divx** – popular codec that compresses video without losing too much quality. Gained some notoriety after it was widely used to distribute movies over the internet.

**WMV** – Windows Media Video. Digital video format developed by Microsoft.

**Xvid** – an open-source video codec, has overtaken Divx recently as the format of choice for sending video over the internet.

## Important

Like digital audio files, videos come in many different formats. Although you can play basic WMV and MPG movies through Windows, you'll need to download alternative codecs to play others. Many .AVI video files use the Divx (www.divx.com) or Xvid (www.xvid.org) codecs and while Windows Media Player can open these, they won't display without the proper software. If you download a video and get the sound without a picture, or vice versa, it's likely because you have a missing codec. You could try downloading a compilation of codecs, such as the K-Lite Codec Pack, which includes just about every audio and video codec you're ever likely to need. You can find it at http://www.codecguide.com/.

# Playing DVD movies

▶

1. PowerDVD, or your assigned DVD player, will open when you insert a DVD movie disk.

2. In the playback controls, the first two sets of arrow icons move you forward and back through the chapters, the second lower set allow you to go back and forward one frame at a time.

3. Drag the dot around the ring to fast forward and reverse. Clockwise to go forward, anti-clockwise to go back.

4. Shows current chapter and title and time elapsed.

5. Adjust the volume.

6. Take a screen grab. The captured file is copied to the clipboard and can be pasted into an image editor.

7. Go to full screen. You can also double-click the viewing window.

8. Open PowerDVD configuration.

9. Select an alternative soundtrack.

10. Choose Subtitles.

11. Navigate to a menu on the disk.

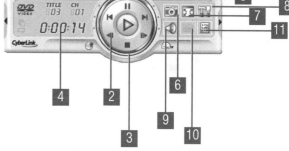

## Important

If you want to play DVDs from a different region, you'll either need to set the region manually or use a software application to disable it. You can find out how to set the DVD region in Chapter 5, but if you regularly play foreign disks it's far easier to use a program like DVD Region Free (www.dvdidle.com) which disables the region and saves you having to set a region on your drive permanently.

We've shown you how to make a slideshow and your own audio disks, so how about your very own DVD? To do this, we'll again be using PowerProducer, the same application used to build a photo slideshow. We selected photos before, so this time we use the Import Video option. Easy! PowerProducer includes some basic options for editing the videos, so you can cut sections, merge clips into one or split them into multiple parts. And of course you can customise your DVD interface as well, making a fully-functional DVD menu that'll work in any player.

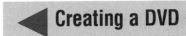
## Creating a DVD

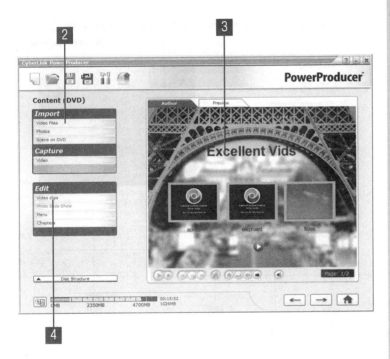

### Select your disk content

1 Following the same steps as we used in the photo slideshow tutorial, open PowerProducer, select Produce Movie Disk from the menu, then choose DVD and set the size of your disk (4.7 GB in most cases).

2 In the Content menu, choose Import Video. Then select the video files you wish to add to your disk.

3 The selected files will be imported and placed in the menu.

4 From the Edit menu, click Video Clips.

## For your information

There are two sizes of DVD disks available – 4.7 GB single-layer and 8 GB dual-layer. Newer DVD burners can handle the dual-layer format and allow you to burn almost double the amount of data. To do this you must have a compatible 8 GB blank disk. To make matters even more confusing, you must also contend with + and – DVD formats. The two types are competing formats from companies that couldn't agree on a single standard back when DVDs were first released. Initially, drives could only handle one or the other, which led to much anger from customers as they bought media for one that didn't work on their single-format drive. All new drives now handle both formats, so as long as you've got a relatively new DVD burner, you don't need to worry about which type you buy.

# Creating a DVD (cont.)

## Cut your video clips

**1** Select a clip from the filmstrip.

**2** Move the sliders on the preview so that they're between the content you want to remove.

**3** Click Delete Selected.

**4** Press Cut to delete.

**5** Click to set the current frame as the thumbnail.

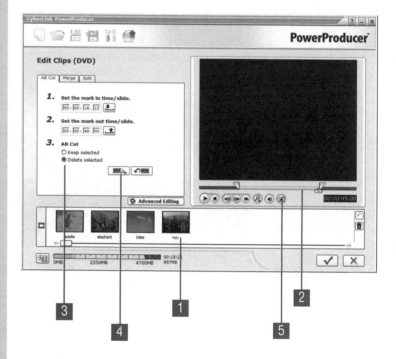

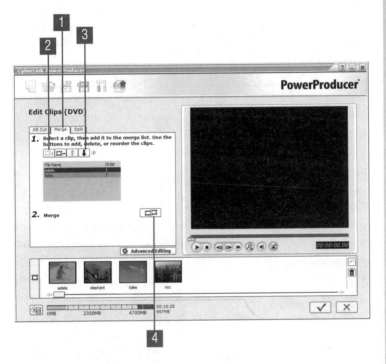

## Merge video clips

1 Click the Merge tab.

2 Use the plus icon to add the selected video clip to the merge queue.

3 Use the arrow buttons to change the order of selected clips.

4 Click the Merge button to join the two clips into one.

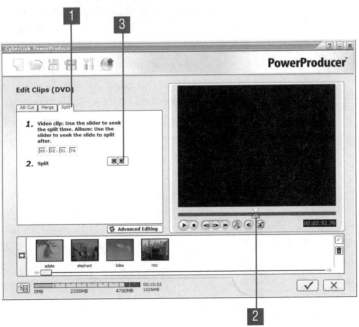

## Split video files

1 Click the Split tab.

2 Move the slider on the preview to the point where you wish to split the video.

3 Click the Split button and one video will become two.

# Finalizing and burning your DVD

Once you've finished adding and editing your video files it's time to customise the interface and commit the contents to a disk. Use the templates to choose a look for your menu and also select a button layout. When that's done, you can create the final product. While usually you'll want to burn to disk straight away, we're going to use the 'DVD Folder' option. This places the files that make up a DVD onto your hard disk, where they can then be burnt to a disk as many times as you like using PowerProducer or any disk burning application, such as Nero. This is useful to know for the future, in case you ever extract the contents of a DVD to your hard disk or download a DVD.

## Edit and test the menu

**1** If you wish to change the template or button styles, click Menu from the Edit section.

**2** To add more video, or even include a photo slideshow, click an option from the Import menu.

**3** Click the Preview tab to view your disk as it will appear in DVD players.

**4** Ensure that you do not go over the maximum file size for your disk type.

**5** Click the Next arrow to go to the final step.

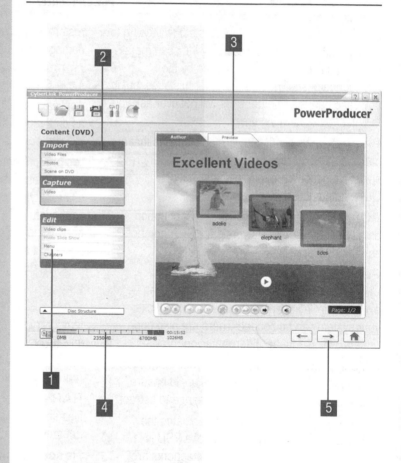

## Finish your DVD

**1** If you're burning straight to disk, ensure that you have a blank disk and that the correct drive is selected.

**2** Click the Configure button to choose another optical drive and change the burn speed.

**3** If the disk is a re-writable, click here to erase it. Note that a number of drives and players have problems with re-writable media, so it's preferable not to use this for video compilations.

**4** You can save the DVD to your hard disk as an image.

**5** For the purposes of this tutorial, we're going to use the Create a DVD Folder option. If you just want to commit straight to disk, select Burn to Disk.

**6** Click Burn to begin creating your DVD.

# Finalizing and burning your DVD (cont.)

## Burn the DVD files

**1** Go back to PowerProducer's main menu and select Disk Utilities.

**2** If you have saved a DVD as image, you can use the Burn From Image to create a disk.

**3** This menu also includes the option for copying a DVD.

**4** Click Burn Disk from DVD Folder.

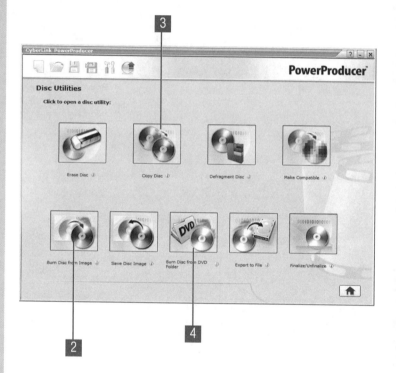

## For your information

The Copy Disk option will allow you to copy a DVD, but it will not work for the majority of commercial disks. Duplicating a commercial disk is a copyright violation and the DVD copying tool will not allow you to bypass the protection that's in place on most disks. There are applications, such as DVD Region Free, that include settings for stripping copy protection from a disk when it's inserted into the drive, but copyright owners have begun to crack down on the companies selling them.

**5** Check that you have the correct optical drive selected.

**6** Set the recording speed.

**7** You can edit the name of the disk.

**8** Click Browse and select the folder where your DVD files are located.

**9** Click the Burn button to create your DVD from the files.

**5**

**6**

**7**

**Burn Disc from DVD Folder**

Drive:

I: PLEXTOR DVDR PX-716A 1.02

Recording speed: 4.0

Disc volume label: NEW_VOLUME

Folder directory:

D:\MyDVD\New

Free space:

Required space: 991 MB

0%

0% 50% 100%

**8**

**9**

# Maintenance

## Introduction

As with any machine, your computer requires regular care and attention to keep it in working order. Unlike a car, you don't need to worry about MOTs and road tax, but you could have huge amounts of valuable data stored on your hard drive, so taking good care of your system will ensure that data remains safe. As well as basic system housekeeping like regularly emptying the Recycle Bin, deleting unused programs and ensuring you have sufficient security, you should use the built-in disk maintenance tools to defragment and fix your drives. There is little you can do about catastrophic hard disk failure, as it will often occur without warning and is often down to a mechanical problem, but you can use these tools to minimise the danger of your files becoming corrupted. It's also vital that you insure yourself against disaster, so we're going to look at the WinZip file compression utility and Windows own Backup Utility. WinZip allows you to create and view compressed archives, which are often used for distributing files on the internet, so it helps to know how to use it even if you never make the zip files yourself. Backup Utility is Windows own tool for making copies of your files. Although most of the applications in Windows are fairly simple, Backup is surprisingly comprehensive and perfect for the casual user so there may be no need to shell out for an expensive specialised tool.

## What you'll do

**Backup your files and folders**

**Restore your files**

**Schedule backups**

**Create compressed archives**

**Use System Restore**

**Defragment your hard drive**

**Clean up your hard disk**

**Perform disk maintenance**

# Safeguarding your files with Backup Utility

Backup, backup, backup. This is one of the basic rules of computing. Hard disks can and probably will fail and you will lose your data, if there are no backups you've got nobody to blame but yourself. There's no excuse either since Windows includes its own Backup Utility. There's no shortage of free and commercial software that does the same thing of course, but since the program is free and will fulfil most users needs it's worth learning how to use it before you consider buying a new package. You can use the advanced mode to manually select files for backup or follow a very simple wizard that takes you through the process and which has options for saving potentially important folders and system settings.

## Backup your files

1. Head to the System Tools menu via Start, Programs and Accessories, then click Backup.

2. Backup starts using the wizard interface but we'll look at the advanced options since they give you more control, so click Advanced Mode.

3. If you do want to use the wizard interface, click Wizard Mode in the welcome tab.

4. The Backup and Restore Wizard are, confusingly, different from using the Backup Wizard mode. They take you step-by-step through the advanced mode.

5. Use the Automated System Recovery wizard to create a disaster recovery toolkit. You'll need a floppy disk and an alternative drive big enough to store the backup file itself. In the event that your hard disk becomes corrupted or destroyed, you can use the floppy to boot up your system and completely restore your drive.

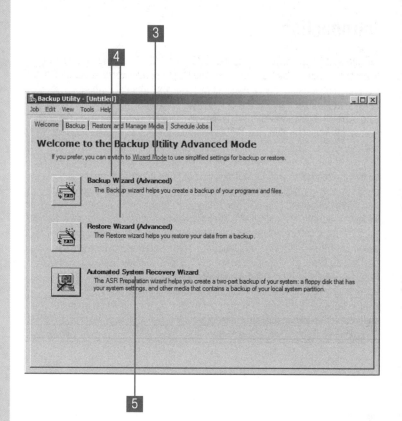

## Jargon buster

**Wizard** – a simplified program interface that makes it easier for beginners to use the application. Although wizard modes often have less features available they're much quicker if you just want to run a basic task.

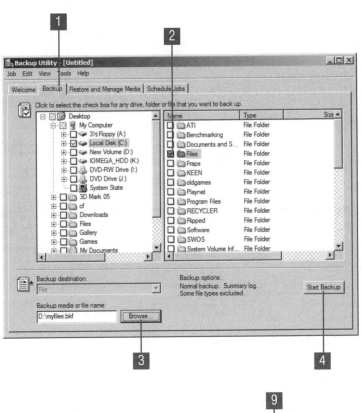

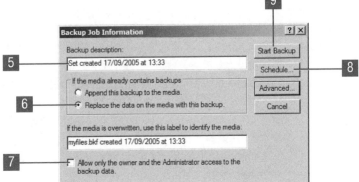

**8**

## Run Backup

1. Click the Backup tab.

2. Browse your system and place a tick next to anything you wish to backup.

3. Click Browse and select a file name and location for your backup.

4. Click Start backup to begin.

5. Enter a description for your backup.

6. Choose whether you want to replace or append existing backups with the new files.

7. Enable this option to restrict access to the account owner and computer administrators.

8. Schedule a backup.

9. Begin the backup process. Your files will be saved to the directory you chose.

### Important

You can swap between different backup types by accessing the options through the Tools menu. In the Backup Type tab you can select an incremental backup that will only backup files which have been modified since the last backup. The Restore tab also has a setting that will overwrite existing files provided they are older than the backup.

### Timesaver tip

Choose the System State option in the backup window to save all your important system settings.

# Restoring your files ▶

**1** Click Restore and Manage Media tab.

**2** Choose a backup file from the list then expand the view so you can see its contents.

**3** Select either a single file from the backup or check the entire folder to restore everything.

**4** Choose whether you want to restore the files to their original location, a new location or extract all files to a single folder.

**5** Click Start Restore to begin extracting the selected files from your backups.

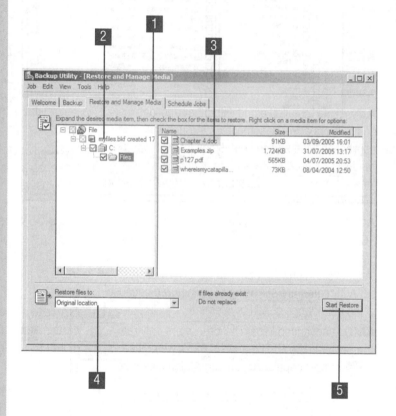

Scheduling backups involves following the same steps as a standard backup, the difference being that you can choose a time and date for the backup to begin rather than having it start immediately. If you want to have a backup run for you later on or at a later date, just set it up and let Windows do the rest. You can even have the backup run regularly instead of a one-off, which is very useful for safeguarding your data.

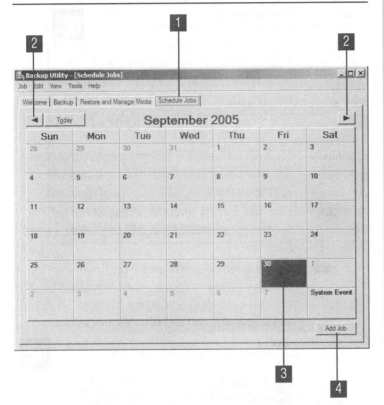

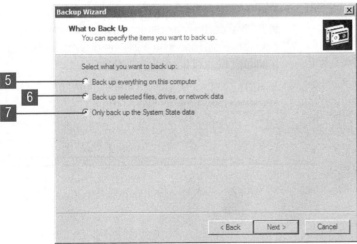

◀ **Scheduling Backups**

## Create a new backup task

**8**

1. Click the Schedule Jobs tab.

2. Use the arrows to change the month.

3. Choose the date on which you want to schedule a backup.

4. Click Add job.

5. Select Back up Everything to save the entire contents of a drive.

6. Use the Selected Files option to choose which files and folders you want to save.

7. System State will save important system files.

**Maintenance    223**

# Scheduling Backups (cont.)

8　Click Browse and select a location for your backup file.

9　Enter a name for the backup.

10　Choose verify data to check that the backup matches the original files. This is useful for important backups but it can take a while on large backups.

11　The greyed out options will be available depending on the configuration of your backup media.

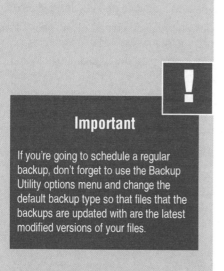

## Important

If you're going to schedule a regular backup, don't forget to use the Backup Utility options menu and change the default backup type so that files that the backups are updated with are the latest modified versions of your files.

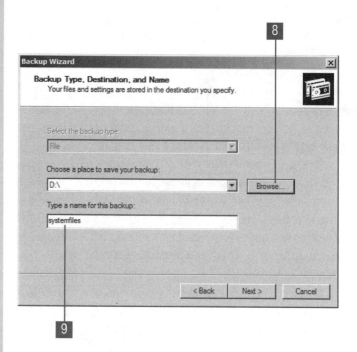

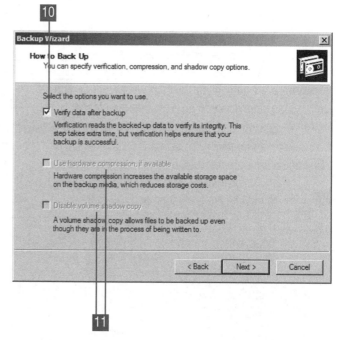

The built-in Scheduled Tasks options included with Windows are used to set a time and date for running your backups. They're extremely comprehensive and will let you run a backup every day, every 5 minutes or once a year. You can also choose to start the computer if it's switched off, stop tasks if they take too long or only start tasks when the computer isn't being used. If you're the forgetful type, this is a really useful tool.

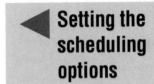

## Setting the scheduling options

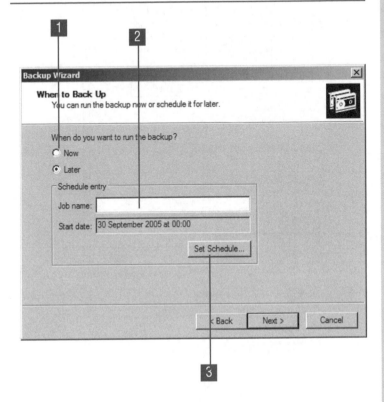

### Choose when to run your backup

8

1 Choose Later to run the backup at the date you previously chose.

2 Enter a name for the job.

3 Click Set schedule to access advanced scheduling options.

# Setting the scheduling options (cont.)

## Change schedule options

1. Select how often you want to run the task.

2. Set a start time.

3. Click Advanced to set the task to repeat every few minutes or hours until a certain point.

4. Select the frequency of the task.

5. Choose which day(s) of the week you want the task to be run.

6. Click the Settings tab.

7. Choose whether you want the task to be deleted when it is finished or to be stopped if it runs for too long.

8. Use the Idle Time options to have backup tasks run only when your system is not in use.

9. If you're using a laptop you can stop tasks from running when you're not connected to the mains.

10. This option will power on your PC to run the task, if it's turned off.

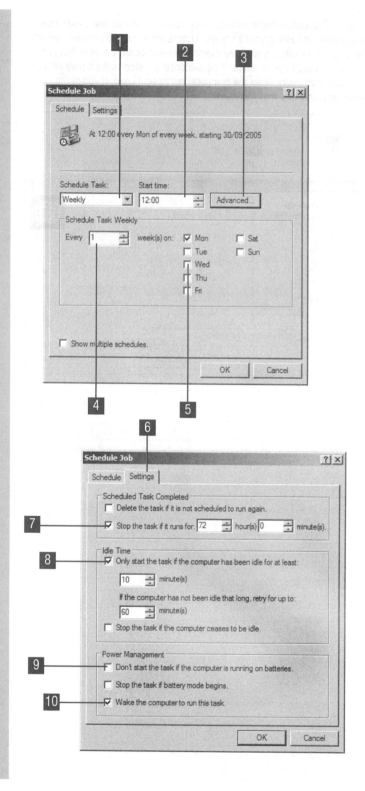

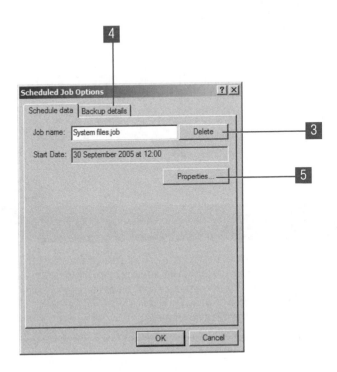

8

### View the schedule

1 Once you've selected the scheduling options and completed the steps, your task will be added to the Schedule Jobs view.

2 Click on an icon to view options and settings for that task.

3 Delete the job.

4 View information about the backup task.

5 Change the schedule settings.

# Compressing and archiving your files ▶

In order to free up some space on your hard disk without deleting stuff, you can create compressed archives by squashing multiple files into single archives. We do this using a compression tool, the most popular of which is WinZip (www.winzip.com).

WinZip allows you to make a 'zip', applying varying levels of compression and other options, into which you can drop any type of file. Compression is particularly useful when backing up (non-vital) files, since you can save space on the backup media. WinZip is one of those essential applications since zip files are used extensively on the internet for packaging downloads. Windows XP does include the capability to handle them without WinZip, but you'll miss out on lots of useful features.

## Create a new compressed archive

1. Load WinZip and click New.

2. Navigate to the folder in which you want to save the new archive and then enter a filename.

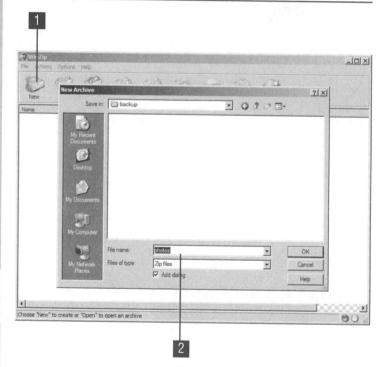

## Jargon buster

**Compression** – the storage of files in a format that takes less space than the original data. For communications, data compression is used to send files quickly between computers while file compression involves squashing a file or lots of files into a single compressed file.

**Zip** – the most popular data compression format. It was invented by programmer Phil Katz in the '80s for his company PKWARE. He also made the first zip file utility, PKZIP.

## For your information

If you download a program from the internet it will often be compressed into a zip file. Sometimes you can run the set-up directly from the zip without extracting all the files, the set-up routine will do that for you, and in some cases you'll need to extract the files to a folder, run the set-up and then delete the original installation files.

**3**

**Add** ? X

Look in: 📁 Gallery ▼ 🕒 🏠 🗂 ▦▾

Desktop

My Documents

My Computer

My Network Places

🖼 pic01.jpg
🖼 pic02.jpg
🖼 pic03.gif
🖼 pic04.gif
🖼 pic05.jpg
🖼 pic06.gif

**7**

File name: "pic06.gif" "pic01.jpg" "pic02.jpg" "pic03.gif" " ▼

Add
Cancel
Help
Add with wildcards

Action: Add (and replace) files ▼

Compression: Normal ▼

Multiple disk spanning: (removable media only) ▼

Folders
☐ Include subfolders
☐ Save full path info

☐ Encrypt added files
☐ Store filenames in 8.3 format

Attributes
☐ Include only if archive attribute is set
☐ Reset archive attribute
☑ Include system and hidden files

**4**

**5**

**6**

**8**

**3** Now browse to the folder containing the files you want to archive and select them.

**4** Use the action menu to select how you want the program to deal with the files. The default Add and Replace will overwrite files with the same name.

**5** Select the level of compression. Normal is the default, Maximum squashes the files as small as they'll go. You can also choose not to have any compression.

**6** Check Include Subfolders to maintain the current folder structure. This means that whenever you extract the files the folder that the originals were taken from will also be created.

**7** Use the Encryption option to password protect your files. You'll be prompted for a password when you click Add.

**8** Add the files to your archive.

### For your information

If you select the Maximum (Enhanced Deflate) compression option, you may not be able to open the archive with some older versions of WinZip.

### Timesaver tip

You can create a zip file from the New menu. Just right-click in a folder or on the desktop, choose New, then WinZip File. Enter a name for the archive and then open it and add files or simply drag and drop them onto the icon.

# Compressing and archiving your files (cont.)

**9** Once your files have been compressed, you'll be taken to the archive.

**10** Files with a wildcard (*) are password protected. When you try to open or extract these you'll have to enter the correct password.

**11** Add more files to the archive.

**12** Click to extract the selected files. You'll be prompted to choose a location for the files. You can also drag and drop files from an archive into a folder but this will remove any folder structure they have.

**13** If you use the Encrypt option here it will protect the whole archive – you cannot select individual files.

## For your information

Although zip files are the most common type of compressed archive, there are many variations. WinZip can open most of these, but it can't handle RAR files. If you need to open and extract an RAR archive you will need to download WinRAR from www.rarlabs.com.

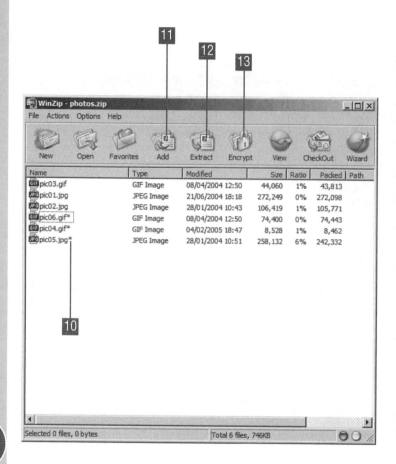

## Important

Don't rely on WinZip for the long-term back up of important files. If a zip archive becomes corrupted you'll lose any data inside them. If you need to backup vital data, consider using a second hard disk, external hard drive or even a RAID 1 (see jargon buster section) set-up, which will ensure that your system is protected against everything but theft or the complete destruction of your PC. Always keep multiple copies of anything you can't afford to lose.

Windows includes a System Restore function for recovering a previous configuration in case you make a mistake or a program goes crazy and starts messing with your settings. System Restore does not affect your saved files but it will remove installed applications and change system settings back to their previous state. This gives you some headroom for experimenting with applications, since you can always jump back a step if it all goes wrong. Helpfully, you can also undo the last restore to set the configuration back the way it was.

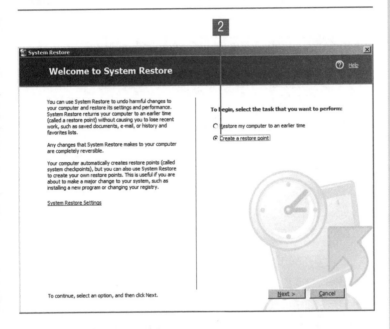

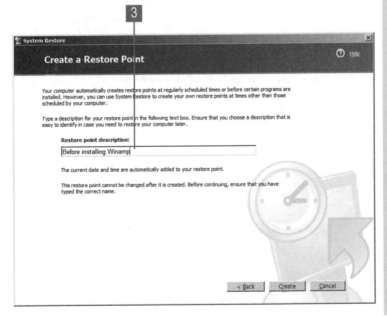

### Set a system restore point

1 Click Start, choose Help and Support then click Undo Changes to your computer with System Restore.

2 Choose Create a Restore Point and click Next.

3 Enter a name for your restore point and click Create. That's it!

**!**

### Important

Before installing any application which could potentially affect the system, such as disk and file management programs or tweaking tools, use system restore and create a backup point. You'll sometimes find that the programs you install have also done this automatically.

# Backup and recovery with System Restore (cont.)

## Recover to a previous restore point

**1** In the System Restore menu, choose Restore my computer to an earlier time.

**2** Click the bold dates on the calendar to see information about the restore points created.

**3** Choose a restore point and then click Next.

**4** Review the information and check that it's correct, then click Next to finish. Your system will now be rebooted and restored during start-up.

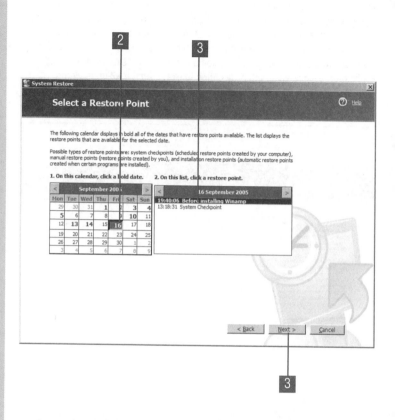

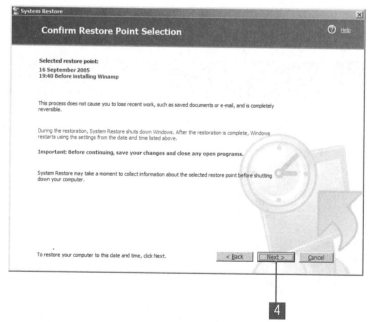

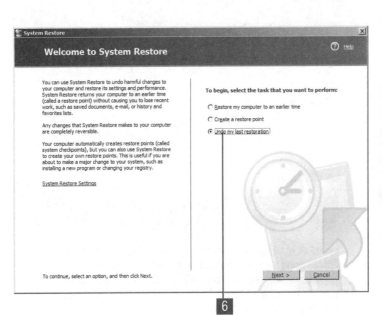

## Backup and recovery with System Restore (cont.)

5 A notice will be displayed when you reboot, confirming a successful restore procedure.

### Undo a restoration

6 Back in the System Restore dialog, you'll have an option for undoing the last restore – this will take you back to the previous settings.

### For your information

Click the System Restore Settings option in the main System Restore dialog and you can change the amount of hard disk space that's assigned for system restore or completely disable the system restore function. Lowering the available file size could cause some older restore points to be removed.

**Maintenance 233**

# Defragging a hard disk

Over time the files on your hard disk will become fragmented, causing the drive to work harder to locate data. Fragmentation occurs when a drive splits files into multiple pieces then uses the file system to track the location of the parts on the disk. When asked to access that file it will need to spend time looking for and gathering the scattered data, therefore it's obviously beneficial to ensure that fragmentation is kept to a minimum so your hard disk will work faster. You should run defrag on a regular basis, about every 1 to 2 months, or perhaps once a month for heavy users. If it's been a while since you defragged you may also need to run it more than once at a time – use the analyze tool to check whether that's necessary.

## Use Defrag to tidy your hard drive

**1** Click Start, Programs, Accessories, System Tools, Disk Defragmenter.

**2** Click Analyze to have Defrag examine the selected hard disk. If the program thinks a defrag is necessary it will prompt you.

**3** After analyzing or running defrag, a graphical representation of the state of your hard disk is displayed here.

**4** View a report that gives detailed information about the current state of the disk. This is enabled after the disk has been analyzed or defragged.

**5** Begin the defragging process on the selected drive. With large hard disks this can take some time, so you may want to go away and do something more exciting or leave it running overnight.

**6** Pause the defrag process.

**7** Stop the defrag process.

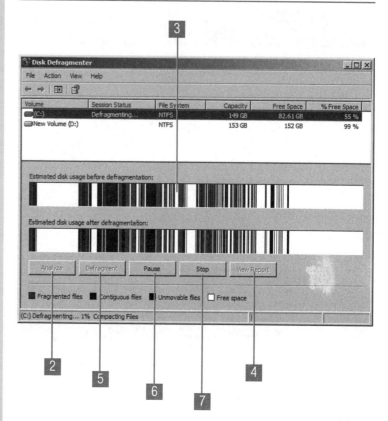

## For your information

Hard disks using NTFS are not as susceptible to fragmentation as those using the FAT32 file system. When formatting a new hard disk you should always choose NTFS unless you have a specific reason for doing otherwise. They will still need to be defragmented, but fragmentation will not occur as frequently.

After a while you'll have accumulated quite a large number of junk files on your hard disk. As well as going round manually clearing up the trash, Windows has a small utility that can scan your drive and pinpoint rubbish. It's useful to run this occasionally as it delves into the depths of system folders and may well find a cache of trash that you would have otherwise missed.

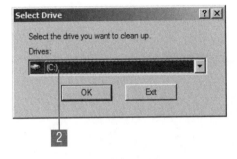

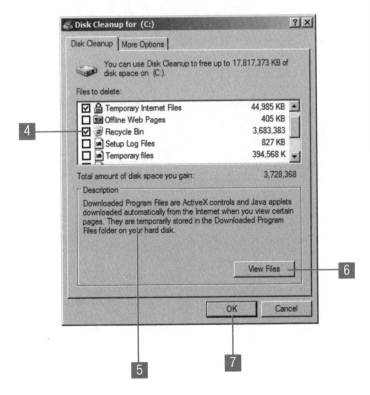

**8**

### Search your hard disk for useless files

1 Open Disk Cleanup from the System Tools menu in Accessories.

2 Select the drive you want to clean and click OK.

3 Disk Cleanup will search the drive looking for files that can be deleted.

4 Check the box next to each type of file you want to clear.

5 Select a file category and check the description that appears to ensure you do not need the files.

6 Click View Files to open the folder containing the selected files.

7 Press OK to delete the checked file types.

# Cleaning up your hard disk (cont.)

8   Click the More Options tab.

9   Windows Components opens up the Add/Remove Windows Components dialog.

10   The Installed Programs clean-up opens Add/Remove Programs.

11   You can also remove old System Restore files. Be sure you no longer need them for recovery before performing this action.

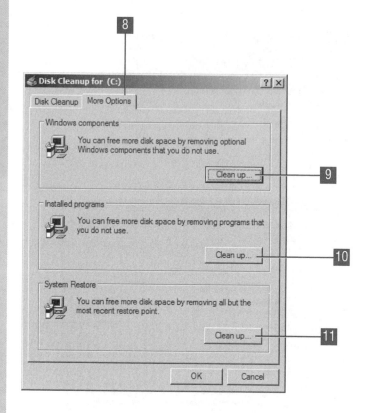

Older versions of Windows and DOS included the Scandisk utility that checked your hard drive for corrupted files and directories. This has now been replaced with CHKDSK. Run from the command prompt, CHKDSK will search for and fix file system inconsistencies which could potentially grow into big problems later on. As with defrag, you should use CHKDSK regularly to keep your hard drive healthy.

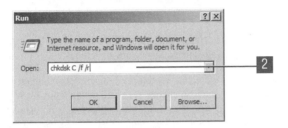

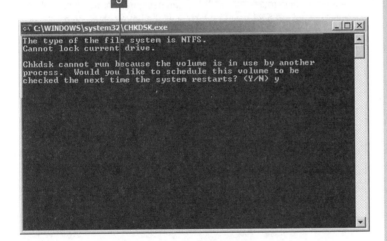

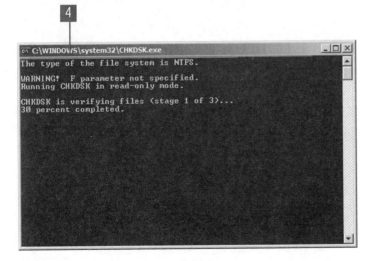

## Use CHKDSK

**1** Click Start, and then Run.

**2** Type CHKDSK C: /f /r. This command will check and fix errors on the C drive. If you want to check another drive, replace the c with the letter of a different disk. Be aware that this process can take several hours, depending on the size of your hard disk.

**3** CHKDSK will ask you if you want to schedule the operation for a reboot, as it's unable to fix drive errors while the disk is in use. Type Y to agree, N to cancel. If you select yes, the utility will run before Windows starts the next time you switch on your PC.

**4** You can run CHKDSK in read only mode by just running CHKDSK C:

Note that it will not fix errors without using the /F switch.

### Jargon buster

**Switch** – command line switches are used to enable or disable options when running a program from the command line or Run dialog.

# Maintaining your hardware

It's obviously not just your software and operating system that needs to be looked after, some TLC for your hardware will also help a computer stay fit and healthy.

- Case fans, CPU coolers and other internal parts will quickly become clogged with dust. If your case has removable filters you can replace or clean them, otherwise use a can of compressed air and blow the dirt out. Always blow it out of your case, never in and do not use the air directly on the fans as you can damage them.

- Make sure that all cables inside your PC are tucked out the way. This will help to keep your system cool by improving airflow.

- Proper cooling is incredibly important as modern components get very hot. If you have a fan hole in your case with no fan fitted, it's a good idea to buy one. Also consider the placement of hardware. For example, hard disks should be as far apart from each other as possible and the same goes for expansion cards. This is especially important when you've got a new graphics card as some of these can get extremely hot, you don't want another card sat right next to it having all the hot air blown on it.

- Ensure that all your expansion cards are seated correctly in their slots and that every component and cable is securely screwed down. The last thing you want is for a component to fall out while your PC is being moved or, even worse, in use. Loose expansion cards and cables are a surprisingly frequent culprit of system errors.

# Jargon buster

**AAC** – Advanced Audio Coding, an audio format that is used most notably by Apple for its iPod audio players.

**Adware** – installed along with other applications and delivers adverts, sometimes through the application window and sometimes through pop-up windows. Often Adware is more of an annoyance than a genuine threat, as many free programs use it to bring in money.

**AGP** – Accelerated Graphics Port, based on the PCI interface, AGP was developed exclusively for graphics cards, replacing the general-use PCI slot. It's now being phased out in favour of PCI-express, but AGP cards are still being manufactured because of the abundance of AGP systems.

**AMD** – Advanced Micro Devices, Intel's only real competitor in the CPU market is AMD, who make the extremely popular Athlon and Athlon 64 series of processors.

**Anti-static bag** – components are usually shipped in grey plastic bags that have been treated to protect against static damage. It's a good idea to hold on to these as they may come in useful when upgrading.

**Associations** – files are associated with applications so that they will open in that particular program when run. This saves you from manually opening a program each time.

**Auto-update** – software that auto-updates will download and install the latest version of itself, often without user-intervention. Sometimes called a live update.

**AVI** – Audio Video Interleave, a Windows video format, used by many different codecs such as Divx.

**Bandwidth** – the amount of data that can be transmitted within a certain amount of time. For internet connections, this is bps, bytes per second.

**BIOS** – Basic Input Output System, the software that enables basic functionality of hardware on all systems, whether they have an operating system or not, and allows you to configure hardware settings. The BIOS is stored on a Read-Only Memory (ROM) chip on the motherboard, so will always be available even if the hard disk crashes. You can access your BIOS by hitting the assigned key when your system starts, which is usually Delete.

**Bit rate** – speed at which data transfers in a certain amount of time. With audio and video files, a higher bit rate means better quality.

**Broadband** – traditionally the name given to a service which uses a single wire to carry many signals, for example cable telephone services that also provide television. Recently it has been applied to fast internet connections though ISPs will call anything from 256k upwards broadband when many don't believe that is true broadband as it's not fast enough. Most broadband connections now are at least 512k.

**CBR** – Constant Bit Rate. If an audio file is encoded with CBR, it means the bit rate, and therefore sound quality, is uniform through the entire length of the file. See also: VBR.

**CDDB** – Compact Disk Database. Many audio

players, such as Winamp, use the online Gracenote CDDB to automatically gather song information. There is also a free competitor, the freedb (www.freedb.org)

**Codec** – COmpressor DECompressor. A codec, such as MP3 or Divx, not only provides the capability to decompress (or decode) files for viewing, but also compress (encode) for creating audio and video.

**Compression** – the storage of files in a format that takes less space than the original data. For communications, data compression is used to send files quickly between computers while file compression involves squashing a file or lots of files into a single compressed file.

**Computer administrator** – when applied to user accounts, the administrator account means that person has full access to the entire system, including the ability to install and remove software and other tasks affecting the administration of the system. When we're talking about networks and corporate computer systems, the administrator is the person in charge of maintaining the systems.

**Context menu** – the term given to the menu that appears when you right-click, so called because its functions change depending on the program or area of the operating system in which you currently reside.

**Control Panel** – an important area of Windows that contains links to settings and controls for hardware, software and peripherals.

**CPU** – Central Processing Unit, often called the processor or chip. It's the brain of any system, handling the majority of the calculations.

**DDR-RAM** – Double Data Rate RAM, the follow-up to SDRAM, this type of memory is currently used in AMD systems.

**DDR-2** – the successor to DDR-RAM. Supposedly faster though there's actually little difference between the two types of memory. DDR-2 is currently used only in Intel systems.

**Defrag** – (defragment) Fragmentation is where files are split into multiple parts around a hard disk. When you defrag, the file system joins these fragmented parts back together, or at least moves them closer to each other, so that the hard disk has less work to do when searching.

**Disk image** – a single file that contains the entire contents of a disk, be it a CD or DVD. You can then burn copies safe in the knowledge that each duplicate will be identical.

**Divx** – popular codec that compresses video without losing too much quality. Gained some notoriety after it was widely used to distribute movies over the Internet.

**Email** – electronic mail, messages sent over an electronic network, stored in a server until the recipient reads them.

**Emoticons** – emotional icons are used in chat to show a particular feeling, like the emoticon for happy :) and sad :( . Often referred to as smileys.

**Enclosure** – also called a case or chassis, it's the metal frame that holds all your PC components together. Cases come in many sizes for different purposes, though the most common is midi-desktop tower.

**Encryption** – the conversion of data into a scrambled code, so that it cannot be read by normal means. Encrypted data must be unscrambled before it can be accessed. Most encryption is not completely foolproof but modern encryption techniques take a large amount of skill and computing power to crack.

**EXE** – a file with the .EXE extension means that it is an executable program file, a self-contained program that will run on its own. This can be a software installation package or application.

**Extension** – the letters after a filename that tell you what kind of data the file contains. For example '.jpg' is a JPEG image and '.txt' is a text file.

**FAT32** – File Allocation Table 32, the 32-bit file system available since Windows 95, which supports hard disks of up to 2 terabytes in size.

**File extension** – indicates to you and the operating system the type of file. The response when the file is opened varies depending on the application with which it is associated. Windows will prompt the user to select an action when unrecognised files are accessed.

**Filter** – a specific pattern or attribute that sorts data based on the parameters given. Think of it like digitally sifting flour, it removes the lumps and only gives you exactly what you want!

**Firewall** – a barrier between the internet and your computer. It protects you from outside threats like viruses and hackers by filtering the incoming data, blocking any potentially harmful information. Firewalls are an absolutely vital part of any system connected to the internet.

**Floppy drive** – or FDD, is used to read 3.5" magnetic media. These disks hold just 1.44 MB so are quickly becoming outdated. Older floppy drives used 5.25" disks.

**Folders** – also called directories, are what Windows uses to organise all the files. Think of them like the filing cabinets in an office, a way of keeping relevant files grouped together for easy access.

**Freeware** – free software. Some have 'Pro' features that are unlocked by paying a registration fee.

**FTP**– File Transfer Protocol, a method for downloading and uploading files to another system over a network. If you're creating a webpage you will usually have to login via FTP to upload the files.

**GIF** – Graphics Interchange Format, pronounced 'giff', commonly used on the web for images because it can be compressed, but not often for photos as it has limited color depth compared to JPG.

**Graphics card** – provides specialised graphics acceleration, allowing for advanced visuals and effects. Using a dedicated card rather than an onboard graphics solution takes pressure off the CPU.

**Hard disk drive** – the primary storage medium for PCs. They are a non-volatile type of memory.

**Heatsink** – used to transfer heat away from components and are often used in conjunction with fans. They're required for CPUs and most modern graphics cards, which run at extremely high temperatures.

**HTTP** – HyperText Transfer Protocol, the system used to display web pages, this tells a server that you're visiting to view a website. Sites beginning with www do not have to be prefixed with HTTP but those without, for example images.google.com, must have HTTP placed in front.

**Icon** – graphical representation of a file or other object. They usually indicate what type of file the item is but can be customised by the user.

**IDE** – Intelligent Drive Electronics or Integrated Drive Electronics, an interface used on CD/DVD drives and hard disks, where the controlling electronics are on the device itself. Sometimes referred to as EIDE, ATA or PATA.

**ID3 tag** – part of every MP3 is given over to holding data about the track, like title, artist, year and genre. This is the ID3 tag. It's used by MP3 players, hardware and software, to display information about a file.

**Instant Messaging** – a method of communication that creates a private chat room between yourself and at least one other person. Instant Messaging can be used to send text or files.

**Intel** – the largest manufacturer of central processing units in the world. The US giant had a monopoly on the CPU market until AMD introduced the Athlon series processor.

**Java** – a programming language created by Sun Microsystems and widely used in websites for features like chat rooms and games, through small Java programs called Applets. Also common on mobile phones.

**Javascript** – not related to Java, a scripting language created by Netscape for the production of interactive websites. It is supported by most modern web browsers.

**JPG** – popular image format, its full name is JPEG or Joint Photographic Expert Group. Often used for photos.

**Jumpers** – a circuit bridge that allows the user to adjust the settings of a device by covering the jumper pins with a plastic plug.

**Kbps** – Kilobits per second, used in reference to audio files to measure the quality of a track. 128kbps is considered CD quality but music fans claim they can hear the difference and prefer songs to be encoded as high as possible. As you increase the kbps the file size also gets larger.

**LAME** – an open-source MP3 encoder. The name was originally an acronym for Lame Ain't an MP3 Encoder. LAME is commonly thought to have the best sound quality of any MP3 encoder.

**License agreement** – the legalese that appears whenever you install software and lays out exactly what you can and can't do with an application. For the average home user there's probably not much of relevance or interest, if you're planning on using a program in a business capacity however you might want to have a read as some free applications require business users to purchase a license.

**Live updates** – allow a program to download new versions of itself or, in the case of spyware and antivirus tools, new information about threats to keep your system protected. Generally, live updates should be done in the background without requiring any user intervention.

**Module** – a program may be constructed from several linked modules, which provide different functions and are themselves small applications.

**Motherboard** – like the central nervous system of your PC, the other components all connect to the motherboard which then shunts data to the correct location.

**MP3** – MPEG audio layer 3, the most popular digital audio format thanks to its ability to compress audio tracks to a fraction of their size without losing too much of the quality.

**MSN passport** – Microsoft's intended 'universal password' system, the idea being that you had one login and password that gave you access to instant messaging, email and websites. It didn't catch on quite as well as they'd hoped however, and has now mostly been diskontinued, though Passport accounts still work to access Hotmail, MSN Messenger and other Microsoft services.

**Network Places** – a central location in Windows that shows your networked drives and computers.

**NTFS** – NT File System, used by Windows NT and later, NTFS offers several advantages over FAT32 such as greater reliability and file and folder security.

**Open source software** – applications where the source code can not only be downloaded but also freely modified, so if you've got the skills you can create your own version of the program.

**Optical drive** – used to read and write to CDs and DVDs. All new DVD drives can read and write both CDs and DVDs. Older drives may be read-only or capable of handling a particular type of DVD.

**Partition** – to divide a hard disk into several individual parts. The operating system then sees each drive partition as a separate disk, as if you had multiple physical hard disks installed.

**Patch** – software updates that fix holes or introduce new features into a program.

**PCI** – Peripheral Component Interconnect, the most common type of interface found on PC systems now, it still appears on the very latest PCI-express boards to support expansion hardware like sound cards, which have yet to switch to using PCI-express.

**PCI-Express** – the 'sequel' to PCI and AGP interfaces, PCI-express offers a (potentially) huge increase in bandwidth. Newer motherboards include one or two PCI-e slots specifically for graphics cards and several more for additional expansion cards, alongside a couple of standard PCI slots.

**Phishing** – a con using fake email and websites that tricks victims into entering sensitive details for online banks and other services such as Paypal and Ebay. The emails often tell you that your account is going to expire and give a link to reactivate. Although the link looks genuine it is actually going to a totally different location set-up by the scammers. Phishing mails can often be spotted by the abundance of spelling and grammar mistakes, but in any case banks and other sites will not ever ask you to enter your details via email.

**Plugins** – additional software applications that are called by a web browser when needed to perform a specific function. Common plugins include Flash, QuickTime and Shockwave.

**POP** – Post Office Protocol, the most common email protocol. The latest version, POP3, can both send and receive email.

**Pop-up** – a browser window that pops up uninvited, usually for advertising. Pop-ups can be extremely irritating and without a pop-up blocker your system can be flooded. There are also pop-unders, which appear underneath your browser.

**POST** – Power On Self-Test, the check that every computer runs when it first powers up, to ensure that all necessary hardware is present and correct.

**Power supply unit** – (PSU) regulates the power to your system. The output of a PSU is measured in watts and modern components are quite power-hungry, so it's recommended that you get a good 350-400W PSU depending on your needs.

**Process** – a program that's currently running. Some background programs are constantly running while you're in Windows.

**Proxy server** – sits between your computer and the server you're trying to access, so the proxy receives the data and sends it on to you. Proxies are often used as a method of anonymously browsing the internet, since the rest of the net sees the proxy details and not yours.

**Quarantine** – when referring to antivirus and spyware applications, quarantine is where all the nasty programs get dumped. A protected area of the hard disk, security tools hold infected files in quarantine so that you can examine them later or restore them in necessary without them causing damage to your system.

**Quick Launch** – a customisable shortcut bar that's enabled through the Start Menu properties. Applications will often place a shortcut here as well as on the desktop.

**RAID** – Redundant Array of Independent Disks, two or more hard disks configured in a way that allows them to work together. There are many different types of RAID configurations, but RAID 1 is very useful for backup since it mirrors the data from one disk to the other, meaning that whenever data is written on one an identical copy is placed on the mirrored drive. If one of the disks fails, you have an exact backup copy.

**RAM** – Random Access Memory, provides temporary storage for files that are in use. RAM is volatile memory and loses the data held when power is switched. Windows and other software require large amounts of RAM to operate.

**RAR** – compressed files. WinZip cannot read RAR files so you must use the WinRAR program or another compatible application.

**Rescue Disk** – provides help in a computer emergency by booting up your system with a variety of diagnostic tools. Many programs offer the ability to create rescue disks, some of which allow you to scan for and clean viruses or restore your computer to a previous state.

**Resolution** – defines the clarity of an image. With monitors, the resolution describes the number of pixels on screen, so a 1280x1024 resolution means that there are 1024 lines of 1280, a total of 1,310720 pixels. The maximum resolution changes depending on the capabilities of the monitor. All new 17–19" LCD monitors are capable of anything up to 1280 x 1024, with larger monitors handling 1600 x 1200 and varying specifications for widescreen displays.

**SATA** – Serial Advanced Technology Attachment, introduced to replace the ageing IDE interface. In addition to offering significant speed increases over IDE, SATA uses smaller cables, which helps with cable management and airflow inside the case. You do not need to configure master/slave settings since each drive has its own cable and numbered socket on the motherboard.

**Shared folder** – one that's accessible to other users of the same computer or network.

**Shareware** – trial software that can be used until a certain expiry date, at which point you must pay to continue using it.

**Shortcut** – link to another location on your computer. If you want to run an application, they save you from navigating to the directory where that program is stored.

**Spam** – junk email, named after the food product or the famous Monty Python sketch, depending on who you ask. Spam has become a huge problem with billions of mails sent every year hawking anything from Viagra to dubious loan offers. Most, if not all, email providers should now have some level of spam filtering.

**Spyware** – applications that monitor your computer and return data about your activities to the people or person's who created them. Often combined with adware. Many spyware applications are malicious, intrusive and incredibly stubborn, proving extremely difficult to remove once they're into your system. In many cases, there's a thin line between spyware and virus.

**Start Menu** – appears when you click the Start button on the Windows taskbar. It's a vital part of

Windows, containing links to applications and various parts of the operating system such as the Control Panel.

**Switch** – command line switches are used to enable or disable options when running a program from the command line or Run dialog.

**System tray** – the area to the far right of the taskbar. It is often used by applications to display status icons, while some programs have the option to minimize to the system tray rather than the taskbar.

**Taskbar** – the bar at the bottom of the display in Windows that stretches from one side of the display to the other. Program icons are shown here allowing you to access any application running by clicking it on the taskbar.

**Toolbars** – groups of related options and tools, usually represented by icons. Toolbars can be floating in a program window or embedded into the top or side of an application window (sometimes called sidebars.) Sidebars are often customisable, giving users the option to disable them or add and remove icons.

**User switching** – an option in Windows that allows you to quickly switch from one user account to another without losing data.

**VBR** – Variable Bit Rate. If you encode an audio track using VBR, the encoder will vary the bit rate (and therefore quality), dropping it during quieter moments. This has the potential to produce audio files that sound the same but that are smaller than those produced with CBR. The drawback is that some audio players are unable to play them back.

**Virus** – software program created for the purpose of causing damage to the system it infects. Some viruses simply damage files, others take over the systems and allow them to be remotely controlled, turning them into 'zombies'. This can be dangerous, as there have been cases where zombie systems were used to store pornography and pirated software without the knowledge of the owner.

**Volatile memory** – like RAM, a storage medium that loses data when it no longer has power.

**Windows Registry** – a database that stores configuration data for Windows, for both hardware and software. You can edit the registry yourself using the RegEdit tool, which is accessed through the Run menu. You must be careful though as mistakes can cripple Windows.

**Wizard** – a simplified program interface that makes it easier for beginners to use the application. Although wizard modes often have less features available they're much quicker if you just want to run a basic task.

**WMA** – Windows Media Audio. Competing digital audio format developed by Microsoft. WMA can include DRM so is a popular format for online stores selling music downloads. Most players support WMA (though some can't read its DRM) but one notable exception is Apple's iPod range.

**WMV** – Windows Media Video. Digital video format developed by Microsoft.

**WWW** – World Wide Web, or simply web. Servers that support a method of formatting documents – websites. Invented by British computer scientist Tim Berners-Lee, the first website went live on the 6 August, 1991.

**Xvid** – an open-source video codec. Xvid has overtaken Divx recently as the format of choice for sending video over the internet.

**Zip** – the most popular data compression format. It was invented by programmer Phil Katz in the '80s for his company PKWARE. He also made the first zip file utility, PKZIP.

# Troubleshooting guide

## Maintenance

## Security

## Software and files

## Windows

# Index